More About SPEAK E-Z CHINESE
Reviews from Advanced Readers' Copies

"A great primer for the slow-to-start – but enthusiastic – all you need to get up and gabbing."
— Sean Moroney, American

"Speak E-Z Chinese has helped me not only to get around big cities in China, but also to bargain with the locals when shopping! It is really exciting for me that I can now pronounce things properly, and I can communicate effectively with the Chinese people! I would definitely recommend this book to people who are just beginning to learn Chinese or to those who want to improve their pronunciation. I found it very helpful during my travels."
— Patricia Edgar, Canadian

"I really enjoyed reading this book. I especially liked the "Go Ahead and Say It" section. I definitely learned some useful phrases."
— Maria Gough, Canadian

"Hey guys – you made speaking Chinese pretty damn E-Z!"
— Robert Henderson, American

Moving to China presents quite a challenge in terms of language. If it wasn't for "Speak E-Z Chinese" we might never have left our apartment! Now we're all over town and loving it.
— Russ and Jodi Riley, American

"Dear Authors: Why not come out with a SPEAK E-Z ENGLISH?" (In Chinese, of course.)
— Violet Liu, Chinese

About The Authors

Timothy Green has been an educator since the word was invented. Besides dabbling in art, he is the author of two children's books and two young adult novels. When Tim isn't teaching, painting, or writing, he can be found working on his Chinese in phonetic English, or practicing not smoking.

Besides interpreting and translating for international schools and companies, Zhao Fang (fondly known as Sam to her friends) has spent countless hours teaching English to Chinese and Koreans, and Chinese to Americans, Canadians and English. Confusing? Not for her. When Sam isn't teaching, she can be found at her computer or playing a mean hand of badminton (that's *yiew maow chiew* in phonetic English).

Also by Timothy Green
    Mystery of Navajo Moon
    Mystery of Coyote Canyon
    Twilight Boy
    The Legend of Wingz

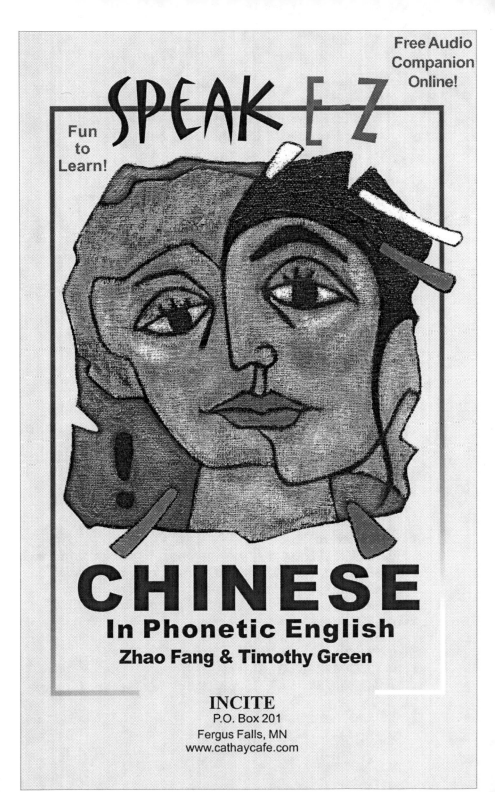

Publisher's Cataloging-in-Publication
Provided by Quality Books, Inc.

Green, Timothy, 1953-
  SPEAK E-Z CHINESE: In Phonetic English / Timothy
Green, Fang Zhao.
  p. cm.
  LCCN 2005907344
  English and Chinese.
  ISBN 0-9771953-0-9

    1. Chinese language -- Conversation and phrase
books–
English. I. Zhao, Fang, 1974- II. Title.
III. Title: Speak Easy Chinese.

PL1125.E6G8 2006   495.1'83421
                                              QBI05-600142

Published by INCITE
P.O.Box 201, Fergus Falls, MN 56538-0201
U.SA
Copyright © 2006 Timothy Green, Fang Zhao

ISBN-13: 978-0-9771953-0-5
ISBN-10: 0-9771953-0-9
LCCN: 2005907344

Illustrations by the authors.

有朋自远方来　不亦乐乎

To have friends from afar is happiness.

- Confucius

Yoh pung zih ywahn fahng lye,

boo ee luh hoo.

- Kohng Zih

Contents

人之初性本善性相近习相远苟不教性乃迁教之道贵以专昔盖

母择邻处子不学断机杼窦燕山有义方教五子名俱扬养不教父

Introduction

Welcome to China, and more specifically, welcome to SPEAK E-Z CHINESE! Whether you are visiting China on business or simply here on vacation, you will find yourself in contact with an enormously rich culture, generous in hospitality and friendship. And although you will find English spoken at many of the finer hotels and restaurants, the language barrier will still be one of your greatest obstacles to overcome. But it needn't be a worrisome problem. By familiarizing yourself with basic words and phrases that you find in this book, you will feel more confident in your interactions with the Chinese people.

SPEAK E-Z CHINESE, by no means, promises its readers to be a comprehensive text for mastering the complex Chinese language. Rather, it can be a valuable tool for speaking Mandarin using an easy to grasp pronunciation guide. Even with a modest degree of fluency, you will feel more comfortable conversing with people while enjoying your stay in China.

For Westerners, the primary fear of speaking Chinese is the usage of the four tones, and yes, tones do, in fact, totally change the meaning of many words. But a great deal of the meaning of any Chinese word is indicated by the context in which it is used, and you will find most Chinese gracious and patient in their communication with you, supporting your efforts to close the communication gap.

The English phonetics used in this book will help you speak the correct Chinese pronunciation, and the downloadable SPEAK E-Z CHINESE audio version will assist you in tonal inflections. *Go-luh!* (That's enough!) So relax, and enjoy your visit in the Middle Kingdom!

▼   Beginning note: For your free audio version, navigate to www.cathaycafe.com: *We're on your way!*

Let's Begin!

I. Pronunciation Guide

It's important to understand that every syllable in Chinese has a tone, which can drastically alter the word's meaning. Mastering the four Chinese tones will take time. For now, let's acquaint ourselves with their sounds, and practice speaking them. We'll begin with the word **ma**. Depending on the tone, **ma** can have four different meanings. For example:

First Tone - mā (mother)	A relatively high level tone, like singing the note "la."
Second tone ´ má (hemp)	A rising tone, as in asking "right?"
Third Tone ˇ mǎ (horse)	A dipping, then rising tone, like irritably saying "So?"
Fourth Tone ` mà (to scold)	A downward tone, like adamantly saying "No!"

About Pinyin Spelling

Pinyin is the official Romanization system of the Chinese language. Most of the letters are pronounced similar to their English counterparts, consisting of an initial (beginning sound) and a final (ending sound).

Initial Sounds:

b, d, f, g, h,	approximately the same as in English
j, k, l, m, n,	
p, s, t, w, y, z	
ch, sh	
c	like *ts* in cats
q	like *ch* in cheap
r	like the *zhr* sound in pleasure
x	like *sh* sound in sheep
zh	like *j* sound in judge

Final Sounds: (with their phonetic counterparts)

a	*ah*
ai	*eye*
an	*ahn*
ang	*ahng*
ao	*aow*
e	*uh*
ei	*ay* as in say
en	*en*
eng	*ung* as in hung
er	*ur*, as in term
i	long e sound, as in ski, except after ch, r, sh, zh, it is *ir*, pronounced with a short i sound, as in sir
ia	*ee-ah*, like the ya in yacht

ian	*ee-en*, like in yen
iang	*ee-ahng*
iao	*ee-aow*
ie	*ee-eh*
in	*een*, as in seen
ing	*ing*, as in ring
iong	*ee-ohng*
iu	*eo*, as in Leo
o	sounds like *wuh*
ong	*ohng*, long o sound
ou	*oh*, long o sound, as in home
u	*oo*, as in moon
ü	*iew*, as in chew
ua	*wah*, as in wash
uai	*wye*
uan	*wahn*
uang	*wahng,* short a sound
ue	*weh*
ui	*way*
un	*wun*
uo	sounds like *wuh*

Standard language texts insist that students initially memorize Pinyin before trying to learn basic Chinese. But good news! With SPEAK E-Z CHINESE, you can by-pass this complex system and focus directly on the phonetic

English. So please take a few minutes to familiarize yourself with the English pronunciation guide below; think of it as a review from grade school days.

ah	as in father
ahng	ah, with ng ending
aow	sounds like the word owl, without the "l"
ay	long a sound, like day
ee	long e sound, like sleep
eh	short e sound, as in let
eye	long i sound, like the word eye
iew	rhymes with few
ir	like sir
lye	long i sound, rhymes with bye
oh	long o sound, like the word oh
ohng	sounds like oh with a ng ending
oo	double oo sound, like moon
tye	long i sound, rhymes with bye
zye	long i sound, rhymes with bye

To ensure that you pronounce the words accurately and enunciate clearly, we recommend that you practice this text with your SPEAK E-Z CHINESE audio version: downloadable for free at www.cathaycafe.com. Remember: *We're on your way!*

万事开头难

Every beginning takes effort.
Wahn shir kye toh nahn.

Communicate

Tohng

II. Key Words & Sample Sentences

■ Pronouns

I, me	**wuh**	wǒ 我
mine	**wuh duh**	wǒ de 我 的
you	**nee**	nǐ 你
(respectively)	**neen**	nín 您
you (plural)	**nee men**	nǐ men 你 们
your	**nee duh**	nǐ de 你 的
your (plural)	**nee men duh**	nǐ men de 你 们 的
he, she, it	**tah**	tā tā tā 他，她，它
his, hers, its	**tah duh**	tā de tā de tā de 他的,她的,它的
we, us	**wuh men**	wǒ men 我 们
our	**wuh men duh**	wǒ men de 我 们 的
they, them	**tah men**	tā men 他 们
their, theirs	**tah men duh**	tā men de 他 们 的

That	**Nah**	那

Who is that?	**Nah shir shway?**	Nà shì shuí 那 是 谁 ？
That is my friend.	**Nah shir wuh pung yoh.**	Nà shì wǒ péng you 那 是 我 朋 友 。

This	Juh	这

What is this?

Juh shir shen muh?
Zhè shì shén me
这 是 什 么 ？

This is Chinese medicine.

Juh shir Johng yaow.
Zhè shì zhōng yào
这 是 中 药 。

■ Interrogatives; 'Because' and 'So'

How
(as in measurement)

Dwuh... 多...

How far is it?

Yoh dwuh ywahn?
Yǒu duō yuǎn
有 多 远 ？

Not far.

Boo tye ywahn.
Bú tài yuǎn
不 太 远 。

How long will it take?

**Yaow dwuh chahng
shir jee-en?**
Yào duō cháng shí jiān
要 多 长 时 间 ？

Half an hour.

Bahn guh shee-aow shir.
Bàn gè xiǎo shí
半 个 小 时 。

How much does it cost? | **Dwuh shaow chee-en?**
Duō shǎo qián
多 少 钱 ?

20 RMB. | **Ar shir kwye.**
Er shí kuài
二 十 块 。

How
(as in actions) | **Zen muh**   怎么

How are you going to tell her? | **Nee zen muh gaow soo tah?**
Nǐ zěn me gào sù tā
你 怎 么 告 诉 她 ?

I am not going to tell her. | **Wuh boo gaow soo tah.**
Wǒ bú gào sù tā
我 不 告 诉 她 。

How do we get there? | **Wuh men zen muh chiew?**
Wǒ men zěn me qù
我 们 怎 么 去 ?

We will take a taxi. | **Wuh men dah dee chiew.**
Wǒ men dǎ dī qù
我 们 打 的 去 。

How do you say _____ in Chinese? | **_____ yohng Johng wen zen muh shwuh?**
yòng Zhōng wén
_____ 用 中 文
zěn me shuō
怎 么 说 ?

What	**Shen muh** 什么

What's your hobby?

**Nee duh eye haow
shir shen muh?**
Nǐ de ài hào shì shén me
你 的 爱 好 是 什 么 ？

Playing guitar.

Tahn jee tah.
Tán jí ta
弹 吉 它 。

What would you like?

Nee yaow shen muh?
Nǐ yào shén me
你 要 什 么 ？

I would like a beer.

Wuh yaow pee jeo.
Wǒ yào pí jiǔ
我 要 啤 酒 。

When	**Shen muh shir hoh** 什么时候

When are you going?

**Nee shen muh shir hoh
chiew?**
Nǐ shén me shí hòu qù
你 什 么 时 候 去 ？

I'll go at 9:00.

Wuh jeo dee-en chiew.
Wǒ jiǔ diǎn qù
我 九 点 去 。

When should we arrive?

**Wuh men ying gye
shen muh shir hoh daow?**
Wǒ men yīng gāi
我 们 应 该
Shén me shí hòu dào
什 么 时 候 到 ？

12

The day after tomorrow.

Hoh tee-en.
Hòu tiān
后 天 。

When will you be back?

Nee shen muh shir hoh hway lye?
Nǐ shén me shí hòu huí lái
你 什 么 时 候 回 来 ？

I'll be back in a minute.

Wuh ee hwer jeo hway lye.
Wǒ yí huì er jiù huí lái
我 一 会 儿 就 回 来 。

Where

Nar / Nah lee
哪儿； 哪里

Where can I find an internet cafe?

Ching wun nahr yoh wahng bah?
Qǐng wèn nǎ er
请 问 哪 儿
yǒu wǎng bā
有 网 吧 ？

Where are you going?

Nee chiew nar?
Nǐ qù nǎ er
你 去 哪 儿 ？

Where is it?

Zye nar?
Zài nǎ er
在 哪 儿 ？

It's behind McDonalds.

Zye Mye dung laow hoh mee-en.
Zài Mài dāng láo hòu mian
在 麦 当 劳 后 面 。

Who   *Shway*   谁

Who is she?   **Tah shir shway?**
                               Tā   shì shuí
                               她 是 谁 ？

She is my younger sister.   **Tah shir wuh may may.**
                               Tā shì wǒ mèi mei
                               她 是 我 妹 妹 。

Why   *Way shen muh*
                               为什么

Why are you upset?   **Nee way shen muh
                               sheen fahn?**
                               Nǐ   wèi shén me xīn fán
                               你 为 什 么 心 烦 ？

Because I lost my wallet.   **Yeen way wuh deo luh
                               chee-en baow.**
                               Yīn wéi wǒ diū le qián bāo
                               因 为 我 丢 了 钱 包 。

Because   *Yeen way*   因为

Why is he so stupid?   **Tah way shen muh
                               juh muh chwun?**
                               Tā wèi shén me zhè me chǔn
                               他 为 什 么 这 么 蠢 ？

Because he has water
in his head.   **Yeen way tah dah naow
                               jeen shway.**
                               Yīn wéi tā dà nǎo jìn shuǐ
                               因 为 他 大 脑 进 水 。

So   *Swuh ee*   所以

I don't have any money,
so she left me.

Wuh may yoh chee-en,
swuh ee tah lee kye
luh wuh.

Wǒ méi yǒu qián
我 没 有 钱 ，
suǒ yǐ tā lí kāi le wǒ
所 以 她 离 开 了 我 。

■ Verbs

Buy   *Mye*   买

What do you want to buy?

Nee yaow mye shen muh?

Nǐ yào mǎi shén me
你 要 买 什 么 ？

I want to buy
a pair of jeans.

Wuh yaow mye
ee tee-aow niew zye koo.

Wǒ yào mǎi yì tiáo niú zǎi kù
我 要 买 一 条 牛 仔 裤 。

And a pair of sneakers.

Hye yaow ee shwahng
ywin dohng shee-eh.

Hái yào yì shuāng yùn dòng xié
还 要 一 双 运 动 鞋 。

Can
(to know how)

Hway   会

He can speak four
languages.

***Tah hway shwuh
sih johng yiew yahn.***

Tā huì shuō
他 会 说
sì zhǒng yǔ yán
四 种　语 言 。

I can speak a little Chinese.

***Wuh hway shwuh ee dee-ar
Hahn yiew.***

Wǒ huì shuō yì diǎn er Hànyǔ
我 会 说 一 点 儿 汉 语 。

I can't sing.

Wuh boo hway chahng guh.

Wǒ bú huì chàng gē
我 不 会 唱　歌 。

Can
(to be able to)

Kuh ee / Nung

可以; 能

Can I return this tomorrow?

***Wuh kuh ee ming tee-en
hwahn mah?***

Wǒ kě yǐ míng tiān huán ma
我 可 以 明 天 还　吗?

Of course.

Dahng rahn kuh ee.

Dāng rán kě yǐ
当　然 可 以 。

I think John can lend me
money.

***Wuh shee-ahng John nung
jee-eh gay wuh chee-en.***

Wǒ xiǎng　　　　néng
我 想 John 能
jiè gěi wǒ qián
借 给 我 钱 。

We can go now.

**Wuh men shee-en zye
kuh ee zoh luh.**
Wǒ men xiàn zài kě yǐ zǒu le
我们现 在 可以走了。

Come   **Lye**   来

Will you come tonight?

**Nee jeen tee-en wahn
shahng lye mah?**
Nǐ jīn tiān wǎn shang lái ma
你今大 晚 上 来吗?

Sorry, I can't.

**Dway boo chee,
wuh lye boo lee-aow.**
Duì bu qǐ   wǒ lái bù liǎo
对不起,我来不了 。

Forget/Forgot

Wahng luh 忘了;
Wahng jee luh 忘记了

I did not forget
your birthday.

**Wuh may wahng jee
nee duh shung rr.**
Wǒ méi wàng jì nǐ de shēng rì
我没忘 记你的生 日。

Sorry, I forget your name.

**Dway boo chee, wuh wahng
luh nee duh ming zih.**
Duì bu qǐ   wǒ wàng
对不起 , 我忘
le nǐ de míng zì
了你的名 字。

We forgot to buy film.

**Wuh men wahng luh
mye jee-aow jwahr.**
Wǒ men wàng le mǎi jiāo juǎn er
我们忘 了买胶 卷 儿。

Give

Gay　　　给

I want to give you
something.

***Wuh yaow gay nee
ee dee-ar dohng shee.***

Wǒ　yào gěi nǐ
我 要 给 你

yì diǎn er dōng xī
一 点 儿 东 西 。

My dad gave this to me.

***Wuh bah bah gay luh wuh
jay guh.***

wǒ bà ba gěi le wǒ zhè ge
我 爸 爸 给 了 我 这 个。

Go

Chiew / Zoh 去; 走

He doesn't want to go.

Tah boo shee-ahng chiew.

Tā bù xiǎng qù
他 不 想 去 。

I've got to go.

Wuh day zoh luh.

Wǒ děi zǒu le
我 得 走 了 。

Let's go!

Zoh-bah!

Zǒu ba
走 吧 ！

Let's go to Beijing.

***Wuh men chiew
Bay jing bah.***

Wǒ men qù Běi jīng ba
我 们 去 北 京 吧 。

Please don't go!

Ching bee-eh zoh !

Qīng bié zǒu
请 别 走 ！

Yesterday, they went to Shanghai.

Zwuh tee-en, tah men chiew luh Shahng hye.

Zuó tiān tā men
昨 天 ， 他 们

qù le Shàng hǎi
去 了 上 海 。

Hate

Hen / Taow yee-en
恨; 讨厌

I hate you!

Wuh hen nee!

Wǒ hèn nǐ
我 恨 你 ！

I dislike you!

Wuh taow yee-en nee!

Wǒ tǎo yàn nǐ
我 讨 厌 你 ！

I hate this place.

Wuh taow yee-en jay guh dee fahng.

Wǒ tǎo yàn zhè ge dì fang
我 讨 厌 这 个 地 方 。

Know
(having knowledge of)

Jir daow　　知道

I don't know.

Wuh boo jir daow.

Wǒ bù zhī dào
我 不 知 道 。

I know.

Wuh jir daow.

Wǒ zhī dào
我 知 道 。

I know how to get there.

Wuh jir daow zen muh chiew nar.

Wǒ zhī dào zěn me qù nà er
我 知 道 怎 么 去 那 儿。

19

Know
(familiar with a person)

Ren shir 认识

I know him.

Wuh ren shir tah.
Wǒ rèn shi tā
我 认 识 他 。

Do you know
Mr. Wang Dehai?

Nee ren shir Wahng Dehai
shee-en shung mah?
Nǐ rèn shi Wáng Dé hǎi
你 认 识 王 德 海
xiān shēng ma
先 生 吗 ？

Know
(closely familiar)

Lee-aow jee-eh 了解

I know my girlfriend
very well.

Wuh hen lee-aow jee-eh
wuh duh niew pung yoh.
Wǒ hěn liǎo jiě
我 很 了 解
wǒ de nǔ péng you
我 的 女 朋 友 。

Like

Shee hwahn 喜欢

Do you like western food?

Nee shee hwahn
shee tsahn mah?
Nǐ xǐ huan xī cān ma
你 喜 欢 西 餐 吗 ？

I like Beijing.

Wuh shee hwahn Bay jing.
Wǒ xǐ huan Běi jīng
我 喜 欢 北 京 。

But I like Tianjin better.

*Kuh shir wuh gung
shee hwahn Tee-en jeen.*
Kě shì wǒ gèng
可 是 我 更
xǐ huan Tiān jīn
喜 欢 天 津 。

I don't like your attitude.

*Wuh boo shee hwahn
nee duh tye doo.*
Wǒ bú xǐ huan nǐ de tài du
我 不 喜 欢 你 的 态 度。

Look / See

Kahn   看

I'm going to Beijing
to see my friends.

*Wuh yaow chiew Bay jing
kahn wuh duh pung yoh.*
Wǒ yào qù běi jīng
我 要 去 北 京
kàn wǒ de péng you
看 我 的 朋 友 。

I'm just having a look.
(often used when
shopping)

Wuh jir shir kahn ee kahn.
Wǒ zhǐ shì kàn yí kàn
我 只 是 看 一 看 。

I saw them yesterday.

*Zwuh tee-en, wuh
kahn jee-en luh tah men.*
Zuó tiān   wǒ
昨 天 ， 我
kàn jiàn le tā men
看 见 了 他 们 。

Love

Eye   爱

Do you love me?

Nee eye wuh mah?
Nǐ ài wǒ ma
你 爱 我 吗？

I love you.

Wuh eye nee.
Wǒ ài nǐ
我 爱 你。

We love to eat
Chinese food.

***Wuh men eye chir
Johng gwuh tsye.***
Wǒ men ài chī Zhōng guó cài
我 们 爱 吃 中 国 菜。

Think

Shee-ahng   想

I think this is rotten.

***Wuh shee-ahng jay guh
hwye luh.***
Wǒ xiǎng zhè ge huài le
我 想 这 个 坏 了。

I think so, too.

***Wuh yee-eh juh muh
shee-ahng***
Wǒ yě zhè me xiǎng
我 也 这 么 想。

Wait

Dung   等

Please wait a moment.

Ching dung ee hwar.
Qǐng děng yí huì er
请 等 一 会 儿。

I'm sorry, I can't wait.

Dway boo chee,
wuh boo nung dung.

Duì bu qǐ wǒ bù néng děng
对 不 起，我 不 能 等 。

You must wait.

Nee bee shiew dung.

Nǐ bì xū děng
你 必 须 等 。

We waited for
the whole afternoon.

Wuh men dung luh
ee guh shee-ah woo.

Wǒ men děng le yí gè xià wǔ
我 们 等 了一个 下 午。

Want

Shee-ahng yaow / Yaow
想要；要

What do you want?

Nee men yaow shen muh?

Nǐ men yào shén me
你 们 要 什 么 ？

I don't want to
buy anything.

Wuh boo shee-ahng
mye shen muh.

Wǒ bù xiǎng mǎi shén me
我 不 想 买 什 么 。

I want some condoms.

Wuh shee-ahng yaow
bee ywin taow.

Wǒ xiǎng yào bì yùn tào
我 想 要 避 孕 套 。

Worry

Dahn sheen   担心

▼ **Note:** When you use *don't* at the beginning of a statement, you say *bee-eh* instead of the common negative indicator *boo*.

Don't worry! **Bee-eh dahn sheen!**
Bié dān xīn
别 担 心 。

She worries too much. **Tah dahn sheen duh tye dwuh luh.**
Tā dān xīn de tài duō le
她 担 心 的 太 多 了 。

Would like

Shee-ahng yaow 想要

I would like a cup of coffee. **Wuh shee-ahng yaow ee bay kah fay.**
Wǒ xiǎng yào yì bēi kā fēi
我 想 要 一 杯 咖 啡 。

Would like to

Shee-ahng... 想

I would like to live in China. **Wuh shee-ahng joo zye johng gwuh.**
Wǒ xiǎng zhù zài zhōng guó
我 想 住 在 中 国 。

■ Quantitatives

Enough

Goh 够

That's enough. **Goh luh.**
Gòu le
够 了 。

Too many / Too much   *Tye dwuh*   太多

There are too many people.   ***Ren tye dwuh lah.***
Rén tài duō la
人 太 多 啦 。

I ate too much.

Wuh chir duh tye dwuh lah.
Wǒ chī de tài duō la
我 吃 得 太 多 啦 。

That's too much!

Tye gwuh fen lah!
Tài guò fèn la
太 过 份 啦 ！

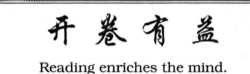

开 卷 有 益

Reading enriches the mind.
Kye jwahn yoh ee.

Revelation

Shir

III. Grammar

English and Mandarin share some basic grammar rules. Each sentence has a subject and a predicate, and the word order is pretty much the same. But there are no verb conjugations in Chinese; verbs do not have to change forms to agree with their subjects, and you simply need to add *luh* or *gwuh* to indicate past or perfect tense. There are no plurals for nouns. Here are some examples:

■ Sentence Structure

Look closely at the basic word order of a sentence spoken in Chinese. First is: **Time** and/or **Place**; next is the **Subject**, followed by the **Verb**; and then the **Direct Object of the Verb**.

Statements:

(Time and/or **Place)+ (Subject)+ (Verb)+(Direct Object)**

Today, at Silk Street Market, I saw Martin.

Jeen tee-en, zye Sheo shway Shir chahng, wuh kahn jee-en luh Mah-ding.

Jīn tiān   zài Xiù shuǐ shì chǎng   wǒ kàn jiàn le Mǎ dīng
今天， 在 秀 水 市 场 ， 我 看 见 了 马 丁 。

Negatives:

Negative sentences follow the same word order, and then you simply add *may* or *boo* (which means *not* or *no*) in front of the verb.

(Time and/or **Place)+ (Subject)+ (***may*** or ***boo*)+(Verb)+ (Direct Object)**

Today, at Silk Street Market, I did not see Martin.

Jeen tee-en, zye Shiew shway Shir chahng, wuh may kahn jee-en Mah-ding.

Jīn tiān zài Xiù shuǐ shì chǎng wǒ méi kàn jiàn Mǎ dīng
今 天 , 在 秀 水 市 场 , 我 没 看 见 马 丁 。

Today, I don't want to go shopping.

Jeen tee-en, wuh boo shee-ahng chiew gwahng jee-eh.

Jīn tiān wǒ bù xiǎng qù guàng jiē
今天 , 我 不 想 去 逛 街 。

Questions:

Questions follow the same sentence structure as statements, and then you add *mah*.

(Time and/or **Place)+ (Subject)+ (Verb)+(Direct Object) +** ***mah***

Yesterday, did you see Martin?

Zwuh tee-en, nee kahn jee-en Mah-ding luh mah?

(Literally: Yesterday, you saw Martin *mah?*)

Zuó tiān   nǐ kàn jiàn Mǎ dīng le ma
昨 天 ， 你 看 见 马 丁 了 吗 ?

▼ Another way you can ask a question is by inserting the negative form of the sentence directly after the positive form, and then you drop the *mah:*

Yesterday, did you see Martin?

Zwuh tee-en, nee kahn may kahn jee-en Mah-ding?

(Literally: Yesterday, you saw - did not see Martin?)

Zuó tiān   ni kàn méi kàn jiàn Mǎ dīng
昨 天 ， 你 看 没 看 见 马 丁 ?

Are you hungry?	*Nee uh boo uh?* (Literally: You hungry not hungry?) Nǐ è bú è 你 饿 不 饿 ?
Are you thirsty?	*Nee kuh boo kuh?* (You thirsty not thirsty?) Nǐ kě bù kě 你 渴 不 渴 ?
Are you tired?	*Nee lay boo lay?* Nǐ lèi bú lèi 你 累 不 累 ?
Do you understand?	*Nee dohng boo dohng?* Nǐ dǒng bù dǒng 你 懂 不 懂 ?

■ Verb Tense & Negatives

Although verbs do not change tense, the modifier *luh* indicates past and past perfect tenses. *Gwuh* indicates present perfect. *May* and *boo* indicate negatives, but they differ with different verb tenses. Examples:

Present Tense:

Today, I go to Beijing.

Jeen tee-en, wuh chiew Bay jing.

Jīn tiān   wǒ qù Běi jīng
今 天 ， 我 去 北 京 。

Present Tense, Negative:

(*Boo* indicates negative.)

Today, I don't go to Beijing.

Jeen tee-en, wuh boo chiew Bay jing.

Jīn tiān   wǒ bú qù Běi jīng
今 天 ， 我 不 去 北 京 。

▼ With the verb *have*, *may* is used to form the negative, rather than *boo:*

I do not have a girlfriend.

Wuh may yoh niew pung yoh.

Wǒ méi yǒu nǚ péng you
我 没 有 女 朋 友 。

I don't have time to look for one.

Wuh may yoh shir jee-en jaow.

Wǒ méi yǒu shí jiān zhǎo
我 没 有 时 间 找 。

Future Tense:

(*Yaow* can mean either *want* or the *to be* verb for *going.*)

I am going to Tianjin.	***Wuh yaow chiew Tee-en jeen.***

Wǒ yào qù Tiān jīn
我 要 去 天 津 。

Future Tense, Negative:

(*Boo* indicates negative.)

I am not going to Tianjin.	***Wuh boo yaow chiew Tee-en jeen.***

Wǒ bù yào qù Tiān jīn
我 不 要 去 天 津 。

Past Tense:

(*Luh* indicates past tense.)

Yesterday, I went to Beijing.	***Zwuh tee-en, wuh chiew luh Bay jing.***

Zuó tiān wǒ qù le Běi jīng
昨 天 , 我 去 了 北 京 。

▼ **Note:** When *may* (indicating a negative) is added to a past tense sentence, the modifier *luh* should be dropped:

Past Tense, Negative:

Yesterday, I didn't go to Beijing.	***Zwuh tee-en, wuh may chiew Bay jing.***

Zuó tiān wǒ méi qù Běi jīng
昨 天 , 我 没 去 北 京 。

Present Perfect Tense:

(*Gwuh* indicates present perfect tense.)

I have been to Beijing. *Wuh chiew gwuh Bay jing.*

Wǒ qù guò Běi jīng

我 去 过 北 京 。

▼ **Again note:** When *may* is added to a present perfect tense sentence, the modifier *gwuh* is kept:

Present Perfect, Negative:

I have not been   *Wuh may chiew gwuh*
to Beijing.   *Bay jing.*

Wǒ méi qù guò Běi jīng

我 没 去 过 北 京 。

Past Perfect Tense:

(*Luh* indicates past perfect tense.)

I had gone to Canada. *Wuh chiew luh*
                       Jee-ah nah dah.

Wǒ qù le Jiā ná dà

我 去 了 加 拿 大 。

▼ **Again note:** When *may* (indicating a negative) is added to a past perfect tense sentence, the modifier *luh* should be dropped:

Past Perfect, Negative:

I had not gone   *Wuh may chiew*
to Canada.   *Jee-ah nah dah.*

Wǒ méi qù Jiā ná dà

我 没 去 加 拿 大 。

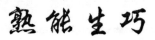

Practice makes perfect.
Shoo nung shung chee-aow.

Harmony

Rohng

Common Expressions
In Alphabetical Order

Almost.

Chah boo dwuh.
Chà bu duō
差 不 多 。

Cheers!

Gahn bay!
Gān bēi
干杯 !

Come in.

Jeen lye.
Jìn lái
进来 。

Congratulations!

Gohng shee!
Gōng xǐ
恭 喜 !

Correct.

Dway.
Duì
对 。

Do you have_____?

Nee yoh _____ mah?
Nǐ yǒu   ma
你 有 _____吗 ？

a lighter

dah hwuh jee
dǎ huǒ jī
打 火 机

an ashtray

yahn hway gahng
yān huī gāng
烟 灰 缸

chewing gum

koh shee-ahng tahng
kǒu xiāng táng
口 香 糖

cigarettes	**yahn** yān 烟
coffee	**kah fay** kā fēi 咖 啡
tea	**chah** chá 茶
tissue	**mee-en jeen jir** miàn jīn zhǐ 面 巾 纸
toilet paper	**way shung jir** wèi shēng zhǐ 卫 生 纸
Do you speak English?	**Nee shwuh Ying yiew mah?** Nǐ shuō Yīng yǔ ma 你 说 英 语 吗 ?
Do you understand?	**Ming bye mah?** Míng bai ma 明 白 吗 ?
I understand.	**Wuh ming bye.** Wǒ míng bai 我 明 白 。
I don't understand you.	**Wuh ting boo dohng.** Wǒ tīng bù dǒng 我 听 不 懂 。
Could you please speak more slowly?	**Ching nee shwuh mahn dee-en, haow mah?** Qǐng nǐ shuō màn diǎn hǎo ma 请 你 说 慢 点 , 好 吗?

Excuse me.

Dway boo chee.
Duì bu qǐ
对 不 起 。

Figure it out.

Shee-ahng bahn fah.
Xiǎng bàn fǎ
想　办　法 。

Good-bye.

Zye jee-en.
Zài jiàn
再　见 。

Good Morning.

Zaow shahng haow.
Zǎo shang hǎo
早　上　好 。

Happy birthday!

Shung rr kwye luh!
Shēng rì kuài lè
生　日　快　乐 ！

Happy New Year!

Sheen nee-en kwye luh!
Xīn nián kuài lè
新　年　快　乐 ！

Happy Chinese Lunar
New Year!

Gwuh nee-en haow!
Guò nián hǎo
过　年　好 ！

Have you eaten?
(traditional greeting)

Chir luh mah?
Chī le ma
吃　了　吗 ？

Hello.

Nee haow.
Nǐ hǎo
你 好 。

How are you? | **Nee haow mah?**
Nǐ hǎo ma
你 好 吗 ？

Fine, thank you. | **Hen haow, shee-eh shee-eh.**
Hěn hǎo   xiè xie
很 好 ， 谢 谢 。

And you? | **Nee nuh?**
Nǐ ne
你 呢 ？

I'm _____. | **Wuh shir_____.**
Wǒ shì
我 是 _____。

American | **May gwuh ren**
Měi guó rén
美 国 人

Australian | **Aow dah lee yah ren**
Ao dà lì yà rén
澳 大 利 亚 人

British | **Ying gwuh ren**
Yīng guó rén
英 国 人

Canadian | **Jee-ah nah dah ren**
Jiā ná dà rén
加 拿 大 人

I'm going to take a walk. | **Wuh chiew zoh zoh.**
Wǒ qù zǒu zou
我 去 走 走 。

I'm on...

Wuh zye...
Wǒ zài
我 在 …

I'm on a train.

Wuh zye hwuh chuh shahng.
Wǒ zài huǒ chē shang
我 在 火 车 上 。

I'm on vacation.

Wuh zye doo jee-ah.
Wǒ zài dù jià
我 在 度 假 。

I'm sorry.

Dway boo chee.
Duì bu qǐ
对 不 起 。

It doesn't matter.

May shir.
Méi shì
没 事 。

It's all right.

May gwahn shee.
Méi guān xi
没 关 系 。

Do you want it?

Yaow mah?
Yào ma
要 吗 ？

No, thank you.

Boo yaow, shee-eh shee-eh.
Bú yào xiè xie
不 要 ， 谢 谢 。

I know.

Wuh jir daow.
Wǒ zhī dào
我 知 道 。

I don't know.

Wuh boo jir daow.
Wǒ bù zhī dào
我 不 知 道 。

I think so.

Wuh shee-ahng shir.
Wǒ xiǎng shì
我 想 是 。

I don't think so.

Wuh boo juh muh shee-ahng.
Wǒ bú zhè me xiǎng
我 不 这 么 想 。

Is it all right?

Kuh ee mah?
Kě yǐ ma
可 以 吗 ？

Yes, of course.

Dahng rahn.
Dāng rán
当 然 。

Just a moment.

Dung ee shee-ah.
Děng yí xià
等 一 下 。

Merry Christmas!

Shung dahn kwye luh!
Shèng dàn kuài lè
圣 诞 快 乐 ！

My name is _____.

Wuh jee-aow _____.
Wǒ jiào
我 叫 _____ 。

Never mind.

Swahn luh.
Suàn le
算 了 。

No problem.   ***May wen tee.***
               Méi wèn tí
               没 问 题 。

Okay, good.   ***Haow.***
               Hǎo
               好 。

Okay?   ***Haow mah?***
               Hǎo ma
               好 吗 ？

Please.   ***Ching.***
               Qǐng
               请 。

Please say it again.   ***Ching zye shwuh ee bee-en.***
                        Qǐng zài shuō yí biàn
                        请 再 说 一 遍 。

Really?   ***Jen duh?***
               Zhēn de
               真 的 ？

See you.   ***Zye jee-en.***
               Zài jiàn
               再 见 。

See you later.   ***Ee hwer jee-en.***
                  Yí huì er jiàn
                  一 会 儿 见 。

Thank you.   ***Shee-eh shee-eh nee.***
              Xiè xie nǐ
              谢 谢 你 。

You're welcome.   ***Boo kuh chee.***
                   Bú kè qi
                   不 客 气 。

This is my _____.   ***Juh shir wuh _____.***
Zhè shì wǒ
这 是 我 _____ 。

boyfriend   ***nahn pung yoh***
nán péng you
男 朋 友

friend   ***pung yoh***
péng you
朋 友

girlfriend   ***niew pung yoh***
nǚ péng you
女 朋 友

husband   ***jahng foo***
zhàng fu
丈 夫

wife   ***tye tye***
tài tai
太 太

What?   ***Shen muh?***
Shén me
什 么 ？

What's the problem?   ***Zen muh luh?***
Zěn me le
怎 么 了 ？

Nothing.   ***May shir.***
Méi shì
没 事 。

Where are you going?   ***Nee chiew nahr?***
Nǐ qù nǎ er
你 去 哪 儿 ？

I'm going to _____.

Wuh chiew _____.
Wǒ qù
我 去_____。

Where can I find a/an____.

Chingwen, nahr yoh_____?
(May I ask, where is ____?)
Qǐng wèn   nǎ ér yǒu
请 问 ，哪 儿 有 _____?

ATM machine

zih dohng chiew kwahn jee
zì dòng qǔ kuǎn jī
自 动 取 款 机

bank

yeen hahng
yín háng
银 行

department store

bye hwuh shahng dee-en
bǎi huò shāng diàn
百 货 商 店

disco bar

dee ting
dí tīng
迪 厅

hospital

ee ywahn
yī yuàn
医 院

internet café

wahng bah
wǎng bā
网 吧

KFC

Ken duh jee
Kěn dé jī
肯 德 鸡

43

McDonalds	***Mye dahng laow***
	Mài dāng láo
	麦 当 劳

park	***gohng ywahn***
	gōng yuán
	公 园

police station	***pye choo swuh***
	pài chū suǒ
	派 出 所

post office	***yoh jiew***
	yóu jú
	邮 局

toilet	***tsuh swuh***
	cè suǒ
	厕 所

western restaurant	***shee tsahn ting***
	xī cān tīng
	西 餐 厅

一把钥匙开一把锁

Open different locks with different keys.
Ee bah yaow shir kye ee bah swuh.

The Way

Daow

Chinese Finger Counting

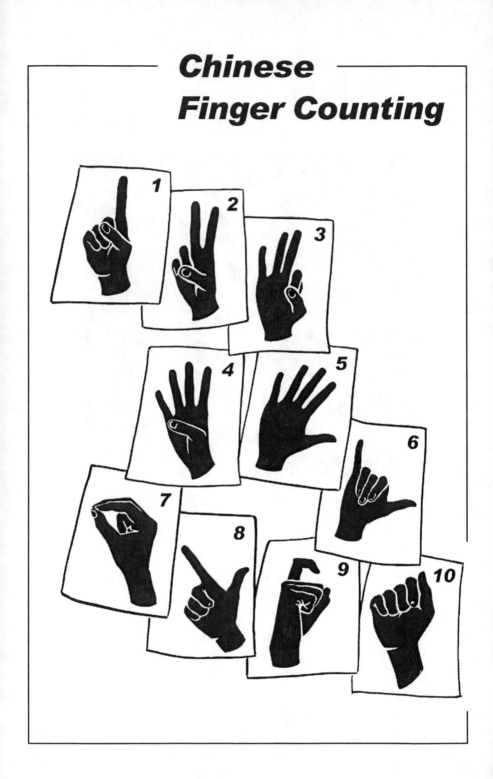

V. Numbers, Counting & Currency

There are special measure words used for counting people or other things in Chinese. The most common of these words is **guh,** which can be used as a universal indicator. (Note the examples under Indefinite Quantities.)

0	**ling**	líng 零
1	**ee**	yī 一
2	**ar** or **lee-ahng**	èr 二; liǎng 两
3	**sahn**	sān 三
4	**sih**	sì 四
5	**woo**	wǔ 五
6	**leo**	liù 六
7	**chee**	qī 七
8	**bah**	bā 八
9	**jeo**	jiǔ 九
10	**shir**	shí 十
11	**shir ee**	shí yī 十 一
12	**shir ar**	shí èr 十 二
20	**ar shir** (Literally: two-tens)	èr shí 二 十

21	*ar shir ee* (Literally: two tens-one)	èr shí yī 二 十 一
22	*ar shir ar* (two tens-two)	èr shí èr 二 十 二
23	*ar shir sahn* (two tens-three This format continues all the way through *ar shir jeo* [29], and throughout all number groups.)	èr shí sān 二 十 三
30	*sahn shir*	sān shí 三 十
31	*sahn shir ee*	sān shí yī 三 十 一
100	*ee bye*	yì bǎi 一 百
101	*ee bye ling ee* (Literally: one-hundred- zero-one)	yì bǎi líng yī 一 百 零 一
102	*ee bye ling ar* (one-hundred- zero-two)	yì bǎi líng èr 一 百 零 二
110	*ee bye ee shir*	yì bǎi yī shí 一 百 一 十
111	*ee bye ee shir ee*	yì bǎi yī shí yī 一 百 一 十 一
112	*ee bye ee shir ar*	yì bǎi yī shí èr 一 百 一 十 二
120	*ee bye ar shir*	yì bǎi èr shí 一 百 二 十

121	*ee bye ar shir ee*	yì bǎi èr shí yī 一 百 二 十 一
200	*ar bye* or	èr bǎi 二 百 ;
	lee-ahng bye	liǎng bǎi 两 百
300	*sahn bye*	sān bǎi 三 百
1,000	*ee chee-en*	yì qiān 一 千
2,000	*lee-ahng chee-en*	liǎng qiān 两 千
10,000	*ee wahn*	yí wàn 一 万
20,000	*lee-ahng wahn*	liǎng wàn 两 万
100,000	*shir wahn*	shí wàn 十 万
1,000,000	*ee bye wahn*	yì bǎi wàn 一 百 万

■ Indefinite Quantities

several	*jee guh*	jǐ gè 几 个
more than ten	*shir jee guh*	shí jǐ gè 十 几 个
dozens of	*jee shir guh*	jǐ shí gè 几 十 个
decades	*jee shir nee-en*	jǐ shí nián 几 十 年
hundreds of	*jee bye guh*	jǐ bǎi gè 几 百 个
thousands of	*jee chee-en guh*	jǐ qiān gè 几 千 个
millions of	*jee bye wahn guh*	jǐ bǎi wàn gè 几 百 万 个

■ Currency

Chinese currency is called **ren meen bee**. The RMB dollar, **ywahn**, is often referred to as a **kwye**, literally meaning a "unit." A **kwye** consists of 100 **fen**, or 10 **jee-aow**. **Jee-aow** are commonly called **maow**.

cent	**fen**	fēn 分
¥.01 (1 cent)	**ee fen**	yì fēn 一 分
¥.10 (10 cents)	**ee maow**	yì máo 一 毛
¥1	**ee kwye**	yí kuài 一 块
¥1.2	**ee kwye ar**	yí kuài èr 一 块 二
¥2.3	**lee-ahng kwye sahn**	liǎng kuài sān 两 块 三
¥11	**shir ee kwye**	shí yī kuài 十 一 块
¥12	**shir ar kwye**	shí èr kuài 十 二 块
¥12.5	**shir ar kwye woo**	shí èr kuài wǔ 十 二 块 五
¥115	**ee bye ee shir**	yì bǎi yī shí 一 百 一 十
	woo kwye	wǔ kuài 五 块
¥230	**ar bye**	èr bǎi 二 百
	sahn shir kwye	sān shí kuài 三 十 块

来得容易, 去得快

Easy come, easy go.
Lye duh rohng ee, chiew duh kwye.

Destiny

Ming

VI. Time & Calendar

■ Time

For telling time, the Chinese say the number and add the word **dee-en**, which basically means "point of time." To mark the half hour, simply add the word **bahn,** which means "half."

early	*zaow*	zǎo 早
late	*wahn*	wǎn 晚
hour	*shee-aow shir*	xiǎo shi 小 时
minute	*fen johng*	fēn zhōng 分 钟
What time?	*Jee dee-en?*	Jǐ diǎn 几 点 ?
When?	*Shen muh*	Shén me 什 么
	shir hoh?	shí hòu 时 候 ?

Early Morning   *Ling-chen*   凌晨
(12:00 A.M. until dawn)

1:00 A.M.   ***ling chen ee dee-en***
líng chén yī diǎn
凌 晨 一 点

2:10 A.M.   ***ling chen lee-ahng dee-en shir fen***
líng chén liǎng diǎn shí fēn
凌 晨 两 点 十 分

3:15 A.M.   *ling chen sahn dee-en shir woo fen*
líng chén sān diǎn shí wǔ fēn
凌 晨 三 点 十 五 分

Or: a quarter after 3:00 A.M.
ling chen sahn dee-en ee kuh
líng chén sān diǎn yí kè
凌 晨 三 点 一 刻

3: 45 A.M.   *ling chen sahn dee-en*
sih shir woo fen
líng chén sān diǎn sì shí wǔ fēn
凌 晨 三 点 四 十 五 分

Or: A quarter to four.
chah ee kuh sih dee-en
chà yí kè sì diǎn
差 一 刻 四 点

4:30 A.M.   *ling chen sih dee-en bahn*
líng chén sì diǎn bàn
凌 晨 四 点 半

Morning   *zaow shahng*   早上
(dawn until noon)

6:00 A.M.   *zaow shahng leo dee-en*
zǎo shang liù diǎn
早 上 六 点

7:15 A.M.   *zaow shahng chee dee-en*
shir woo (fen)
zǎo shang qī diǎn shí wǔ fēn
早 上 七 点 十 五 （分）

8:40 A.M.	***zaow shahng bah dee-en sih shir (fen)*** zǎo shang bā diǎn sì shí fēn 早 上 八 点 四 十（分）
9:45 A.M.	***zaow shahng jeo dee-en sih shir woo (fen)*** zǎo shang jiǔ diǎn sì shí wǔ fēn 早 上 九 点 四 十 五（分）
10:50 A.M.	***zaow shahng shir dee-en woo shir (fen)*** zǎo shang shí diǎn wǔ shí fēn 早 上 十 点 五 十（分）

Noon　　　　　*Johng woo*　　中午

12:00 noon	***johng woo shir ar dee-en*** zhōng wǔ shí èr diǎn 中 午 十 二 点
12:15 P.M.	***johng woo shir ar dee-en ee kuh*** zhōng wǔ shí èr diǎn yí kè 中 午 十 二 点 一 刻

Afternoon　　　*Shee-ah woo*　　下午

1:00 P.M.	***shee-ah woo ee dee-en*** xià wǔ yī diǎn 下 午 一 点
2:30 P.M.	***shee-ah woo lee-ahng dee-en sahn shir (fen)*** xià wǔ liǎng diǎn sān shí fēn 下 午 两 点 三 十（分）

3:50 P.M.	***shee-ah woo sahn dee-en woo shir (fen)***	

xià wǔ   sān diǎn wǔ shí   fēn
下 午 三 点 五 十（分）

Evening and Night   ***Wahn shahng***   晚上

6:30 P.M.	***wahn shahng leo dee-en bahn***

wǎn shang liù diǎn bàn
晚 上 六 点 半

7:00 P.M.	***wahn shahng chee dee-en***

wǎn shang qī diǎn
晚 上 七 点

9:15 P.M.	***wahn shahng jeo dee-en shir woo (fen)***

wǎn shang jiǔ diǎn shí wǔ   fēn
晚 上 九 点 十 五（分）

■ Calendar

day	***tee-en***	tiān 天
today	***jeen tee-en***	jīn tiān 今 天
tomorrow	***ming tee-en***	míng tiān 明 天
the day after tomorrow	***hoh tee-en***	hòu tiān 后 天
three days from now	***dah hoh tee-en***	dà hòu tiān 大 后 天
yesterday	***zwuh tee-en***	zuó tiān 昨 天

the day before yesterday	*chee-en tee-en*	qián tiān 前 天

Counting days

1 day	*ee tee-en*	yì tiān 一 天
2 days	*lee-ahng tee-en*	liǎng tiān 两 天
3 days	*sahn tee-en*	sān tiān 三 天

1st day	*dee ee tee-en*	dì yī tiān 第 一 天
2nd day	*dee ar tee-en*	dì èr tiān 第 二 天
3rd day	*dee sahn tee-en*	dì sān tiān 第 三 天

Weeks — *Shing chee* — 星期

Monday	*Shing chee ee*	xīng qī yī 星 期 一
Tuesday	*Shing chee ar*	xīng qī èr 星 期 二
Wednesday	*Shing chee sahn*	xīng qī sān 星 期 三
Thursday	*Shing chee sih*	xīng qī sì 星 期 四
Friday	*Shing chee woo*	xīng qī wǔ 星 期 五
Saturday	*Shing chee leo*	xīng qī liù 星 期 六
Sunday	*Shing chee rr/ tee-en*	xīng qī rì tiān 星 期 日/天

1 week	*ee guh shing chee*	yí ge xīng qī 一 个 星 期
2 weeks	*lee-ahng guh shing chee*	liǎng ge xīng qī 两 个 星 期
last week	*shahng guh shing chee*	shàng ge xīng qī 上 个 星 期
next week	*shee-ah guh shing chee*	xià ge xīng qī 下 个 星 期
this week	*jay guh shing chee*	zhè ge xīng qī 这 个 星 期

Months   *Yweh*   月

January	*Ee yweh*	yī yuè 一 月
February	*Ar yweh*	èr yuè 二 月
March	*Sahn yweh*	sān yuè 三 月
April	*Sih yweh*	sì yuè 四 月
May	*Woo yweh*	wǔ yuè 五 月
June	*Leo yweh*	liù yuè 六 月
July	*Chee yweh*	qī yuè 七 月
August	*Bah yweh*	bā yuè 八 月

		jiǔ yuè
September	*Jeo yweh*	九 月

		shí yuè
October	*Shir yweh*	十 月

		shí yī yuè
November	*Shir ee yweh*	十 一 月

		shí èr yuè
December	*Shir ar yweh*	十 二 月

Specific monthly dates

If you need to state a specific date, you say the month, then the number of the date, followed by the word "*haow*". For example, December 1ˢᵗ is *Shir ar yweh ee haow* (month, number, haow.) Try: September 7ᵗʰ *Jeo yweh chee haow.*

January 1ˢᵗ   *Ee yweh ee haow*
yī yuè yī hào
一 月 一 号

February 12ᵗʰ   *Ar yweh shir ar haow*
èr yuè shí èr hào
二 月 十 二 号

March 20ᵗʰ   *Sahn yweh ar shir haow*
sān yuè èr shí hào
三 月 二 十 号

May 31ˢᵗ   *Woo yweh sahn shir ee haow*
wǔ yuè sān shí yī hào
五 月 三 十 一 号

Years	**Nee-en**	年
1 year	**ee nee-en**	yì nián 一 年
2 years	**lee-ahng nee-en**	liǎng nián 两 年
last year	**chiew nee-en**	qù nián 去 年
next year	**ming nee-en**	míng nián 明 年
this year	**jeen nee-en**	jīn nián 今 年
199__(year)	**ee jeo jeo ____ nee-en**	yī jiǔ jiǔ　　 nián 一 九 九 ____ 年
200__(year)	**ar ling ling ____ nee-en**	èr líng líng　　 nián 二 零 零 ____ 年

天有不测风云

Nothing is so certain as the unexpected.
Tee-en yoh boo tsuh fung ywin.

To Go

Shing

VII. Transportation & Accomodations

■ Airport, Ticket Window, Ticket Agency

I would like to buy _____ plane ticket(s).

Wuh yaow mye _____ jahng fay jee pee-aow.

Wǒ yào mǎi
我 要 买 _____
zhāng fēi jī piào
张 飞 机 票 。

one	***ee***	yì 一
two	***lee-ahng***	liǎng 两
three	***sahn***	sān 三
four	***sih***	sì 四

From _____ to _____.

Tsohng ___ daow ___ duh.

cóng   dào   de
从 ___ 到 ___ 的 。

Beijing	***Bay jing***	Běi jīng 北 京
Chengdu	***Chung doo***	Chéng dū 成 都
Chongqing	***Chohng ching***	Chóng qìng 重 庆
Dali	***Dah lee***	Dà lǐ 大 理
Guangzhou	***Gwahng joh***	Guǎng zhōu 广 州

Guilin	*Gway leen*	Guì lín 桂 林
Haerbin	*Ha ar been*	Hā ěr bīn 哈 尔 滨
Hainan	*Hye nahn*	Hǎi nán 海 南
Hohhot	*Hoo huh haow tuh*	Hū hé hào tè 呼 和 浩 特
Lanzhou	*Lahn joh*	Lán zhōu 兰 州
Lijiang	*Lee jee-ahng*	Lì jiāng 丽 江
Nanjing	*Nahn jing*	Nán jīng 南 京
Nanning	*Nahn ning*	Nán níng 南 宁
Qingdao	*Ching daow*	Qīng dǎo 青 岛
Qufu	*Chiew foo*	Qǔ fù 曲 阜
Shanghai	*Shahng hye*	Shàng hǎi 上 海
Shenzhen	*Shen jen*	Shēn zhèn 深 圳
Taiyuan	*Tye ywahn*	Tài yuán 太 原
Tianjin	*Tee-en jeen*	Tiān jīn 天 津
Tibet	*Shee zahng*	Xī zàng 西 藏
Tulufan	*Too loo fahn*	Tǔ lǔ fān 吐 鲁 番
Wulumuqi	*Woo loo moo chee*	Wū lǔ mù qí 乌 鲁 木 齐
Xi'an	*Shee ahn*	Xī 'ān 西 安

Xiamen	*Shee-ah men*	Xià mén 厦 门
Xinjiang	*Sheen jee-ahng*	Xīn jiāng 新 疆
Xishuang- banna	*Shee shwahng bahn nah*	Xī shuāng bǎn nà 西 双 版 纳
Yangshuo	*Yahng shwuh*	Yáng shuò 杨 朔
Yunnan	*Ywin nahn*	Yún nán 云 南

One way ticket.

Dahn chung pee-aow.
Dān chéng piào
单 程 票。

Return ticket.

Wahng fahn pee-aow.
Wǎng fǎn piào
往 返 票。

I want to leave_____.

Wuh yaow _____ duh.
Wǒ yào   de
我 要 _____ 的。

today

jeen tee-en
jīn tiān
今 天

this morning

jeen tee-en shahng woo
jīn tiān shàng wǔ
今 天 上 午

this afternoon

jeen tee-en shee-ah woo
jīn tiān xià wǔ
今 天 下 午

tomorrow	***ming tee-en*** míng tiān 明 天
tomorrow morning	***ming tee-en shahng woo*** míng tiān shàng wǔ 明 天 上 午
tomorrow evening	***ming tee-en wahn shahng*** míng tiān wǎn shang 明 天 晚 上
the day after tomorrow	***hoh tee-en*** hòu tiān 后 天
___(month)___(day)	___ ***yweh*** ___ ***haow*** yuè hào ___ 月 ___ 号
January 1st	***ee yweh ee haow*** yī yuè yī hào 一 月 一 号
How much?	***Dwuh shaow chee-en?*** Duō shǎo qián 多 少 钱 ?
How much of a discount?	***Dah jee juh?*** Dǎ jǐ zhé 打 几 折 ?
May I pay with my credit card?	***Kuh ee yohng*** ***sheen yohng kah mah?*** Kě yǐ yòng xìn yòng kǎ ma 可 以 用 信 用 卡 吗 ?

■ Railway Station, Ticket Window

Hwuh chuh jahn, Show pee-aow choo
huǒ chē zhàn shòu piào chù
火 车 站 ， 售 票 处

I would like to buy a ticket to _____.	*Wuh yaow mye ee jahng chiew _____ duh pee-aow.* Wǒ yào mǎi yì zhāng 我 要 买 一 张 qù de piào 去 _____ 的 票 。
I would like to buy a ticket from _____ to _____.	*Wuh yaow mye ee jahng pee-aow, tsohng _____ daow _____ duh.* Wǒ yào mǎi yì zhāng piào 我 要 买 一 张 票 ， cóng dào de 从 _____ 到 _____ 的 。

Beijing	*Bay jing*	Běi jīng 北 京
Chengdu	*Chung doo*	Chéng dū 成 都
Chongqing	*Chohng ching*	Chóng qìng 重 庆
Dali	*Dah lee*	Dà lǐ 大 理
Guangzhou	*Gwahng joh*	Guǎng zhōu 广 州
Guilin	*Gway leen*	Guì lín 桂 林
Haerbin	*Ha ar been*	Hā ěr bīn 哈 尔 滨
Hainan	*Hye nahn*	Hǎi nán 海 南

Hohhot	*Hoo huh haow tuh*	Hū hé hào tè 呼 和 浩 特
Lanzhou	*Lahn joh*	Lán zhōu 兰 州
Lijiang	*Lee jee-ahng*	Lì jiāng 丽 江
Nanjing	*Nahn jing*	Nán jīng 南 京
Nanning	*Nahn ning*	Nán níng 南 宁
Qingdao	*Ching daow*	Qīng dǎo 青 岛
Qufu	*Chiew foo*	Qǔ fù 曲 阜
Shanghai	*Shahng hye*	Shàng hǎi 上 海
Shenzhen	*Shen jen*	Shēn zhèn 深 圳
Taiyuan	*Tye ywahn*	Tài yuán 太 原
Tianjin	*Tee-en jeen*	Tiān jīn 天 津
Tibet	*Shee zahng*	Xī zàng 西 藏
Tulufan	*Too loo fahn*	Tǔ lǔ fān 吐 鲁 番
Wulumuqi	*Woo loo moo chee*	Wū lǔ mù qí 乌 鲁 木 齐
Xi'an	*Shee ahn*	Xī 'ān 西 安
Xiamen	*Shee-ah men*	Xià mén 厦 门
Xinjiang	*Sheen jee-ahng*	Xīn jiāng 新 疆
Xishuang-banna	*Shee shwahng bahn nah*	Xī shuāng 西 双 bǎn nà 版 纳

| Yangshuo | **Yahng shwuh** | Yáng shuò
杨 朔 |
| Yunnan | **Ywin nahn** | Yún nán
云 南 |

I want to leave_____. **Wuh yaow _____ duh.**

Wǒ yào   de
我 要 _____ 的 。

today
jeen tee-en
jīn tiān
今 天

this morning
jeen tee-en shahng woo
jīn tiān shàng wǔ
今 天 上 午

this afternoon
jeen tee-en shee-ah woo
jīn tiān xià wǔ
今 天 下 午

tomorrow
ming tee-en
míng tiān
明 天

tomorrow morning
ming tee-en shahng woo
míng tiān shàng wǔ
明 天 上 午

tomorrow evening
ming tee-en wahn shahng
míng tiān wǎn shang
明 天 晚 上

the day after tomorrow
hoh tee-en
hòu tiān
后 天

___(month)___(day)   ___ *yweh* ___ *haow*

yuè   hào

___ 月 ___ 号

I would like a / an _____.   *Wuh yaow _____.*

Wǒ yào

我 要 _____。

hard seat	*ying zwuh*	yìng zuò 硬 座
soft seat	*rwahn zwuh*	ruǎn zuò 软 座
hard sleeper	*ying wuh*	yìng wò 硬 卧
soft sleeper	*rwahn wuh*	ruǎn wò 软 卧
bottom sleeper	*shee-ah poo*	xià pù 下 铺
middle sleeper	*johng poo*	zhōng pù 中 铺
upper sleeper	*shahng poo*	shàng pù 上 铺

一 路 顺 风

Have a pleasant journey.
Ee loo shwun fung.

■ Taxi

▼ *Shir foo* is generally used as a term to address a taxi driver; it is also used to address a Kung Fu master.

Hello (to driver).

Nee haow, Shir foo.
Nǐ hǎo shī fu
你好，师傅。

Hello, Comrade!

Nee haow, Tohng jir.
Nǐ hǎo tóng zhì
你好，同志！

Please drive me
to (the) _____.

*Ching sohng wuh
chiew_____.*
Qǐng sòng wǒ qù
请 送 我 去_____。

airport	*fay jee chahng*	fēi jī chǎng 飞 机 场
train station	*hwuh chuh jahn*	huǒ chē zhàn 火 车 站
this place	*jay guh dee fahng*	zhè ge dì fang 这 个 地 方

Please drive me to
the nearest_____.

*Ching sohng wuh chiew
zway jeen duh_____.*
Qǐng sòng wǒ qù
请 送 我 去
zuì jìn de
最 近 的_____。

bank

yeen hahng
yín háng
银 行

department store	**bye hwuh shahng dee-en**
	bǎi huò shāng diàn
	百 货 商 店

disco bar	**dee ting**
	dí tīng
	迪 厅

hospital	**ee ywahn**
	yī yuàn
	医 院

KFC	**Ken duh jee**
	kěn dé jī
	肯 德 鸡

McDonalds	**Mye dahng laow**
	mài dāng láo
	麦 当 劳

park	**gohng ywahn**
	gōng yuán
	公 园

police station	**pye choo swuh**
	pài chū suǒ
	派 出 所

post office	**yoh jiew**
	yóu jú
	邮 局

western restaurant	**shee tsahn ting**
	xī cān tīng
	西 餐 厅

Please take me to this address:	***Ching sohng wuh chiew jay guh dee jir:*** Qǐng sòng wǒ qù zhè ge dì zhǐ 请 送 我去这 个地址：
Turn on the meter, please.	***Ching dah bee-aow.*** Qǐng dǎ biǎo 请 打表 。
I'm in a hurry.	***Wuh gahn shir jee-en.*** Wǒ gǎn shí jiān 我 赶 时 间 。
Safety is first.	***Ahn chwahn dee ee.*** An quán dì yī 安 全 第一 。
Slow down, please.	***Ching mahn dee-ar kye.*** Qǐng màn diǎn ér kāi 请 慢 点 儿开 。
How far is it?	***Yoh dwuh ywahn?*** Yǒu duō yuǎn 有 多 远 ？
How long will it take?	***Yaow dwuh chahng shir jee-en?*** Yào duō cháng shí jiān 要 多长 时 间 ？
Turn left.	***Zwuh gwye.*** Zuǒ guǎi 左 拐 。
Turn right.	***Yoh gwye.*** Yòu guǎi 右 拐 。

Go straight.

Ee jir zoh.
Yì zhí zǒu
一 直 走 。

Turn around, please.

Ching dee-aow toh.
Qǐng diào tóu
请 掉 头 。

Drive me back, please.

Ching dye wuh hway chiew.
Qǐng dài wǒ huí qù
请 带 我 回 去 。

Stop.

Ting.
Tíng
停 。

We have arrived.

Daow luh.
Dào le
到 了 。

Stop here!

Ting juhr!
Tíng zhè er
停 这 儿 ！

How much is it?

Dwuh shaow chee-en?
Duō shǎo qián
多 少 钱 ？

Here is the money.

Gay nee chee-en.
Gěi nǐ qián
给 你 钱 。

Sorry, I don't have smaller change.

Dway boo chee,
may ling chee-en.
Duì bu qǐ   méi líng qián
对 不 起 ， 没 零 钱 。

I need a receipt.   ***Wuh yaow fah pee-aow.***
Wǒ yào fā piào
我 要 发 票 。

■ Transportation Vocabulary

airplane   ***fay jee***
fēi jī
飞 机

airport shuttle bus   ***jee chahng bah shir***
jī chǎng bā shì
机 场 巴 士

airport   ***fay jee chahng***
fēi jī chǎng
飞 机 场

check-in counter   ***jee-en pee-aow choo***
jiǎn piào chù
检 票 处

check-in time   ***jee-en pee-aow shir jee-en***
jiǎn piào shí jiān
检 票 时 间

customs   ***hye gwahn***
hǎi guān
海 关

departure time   ***chee fay shir jee-en***
qǐ fēi shí jiān
起 飞 时 间

driver   ***sih jee***
sī jī
司 机

English	Phonetic	Pinyin	Chinese

economy class   **jing jee tsahng**
jīng jì cāng
经 济 舱

express train   **tuh kwye lee-eh chuh**
tè kuài liè chē
特 快 列 车

first class   **toh dung tsahng**
tóu děng cāng
头 等 舱

flight ticket   **fay jee pee-aow**
fēi jī piào
飞 机 票

flight   **hahng bahn**
háng bān
航 班

hotel shuttle bus   **jeo dee-en bah shir**
jiǔ diàn bā shì
酒 店 巴 士

passport   **who jaow**
hù zhào
护 照

seats   **zwuh way**
zuò wèi
座 位

take a taxi   **dah dee**
dǎ dī
打 的

taxi   **choo zoo chuh**
chū zū chē
出 租 车

ticket	***pee-aow*** piào 票
traffic jam	***sye chuh*** sāi chē 塞 车
train station	***hwuh chuh jahn*** huǒ chē zhàn 火 车 站
train ticket	***hwuh chuh pee-aow*** huǒ chē piào 火 车 票
train	***hwuh chuh*** huǒ chē 火 车

■ Accommodations

Is there a room vacant?	***Yoh kohng fahng jee-en mah?*** Yǒu kōng fáng jiān ma 有 空 房 间 吗 ?
I have a reservation.	***Wuh yiew ding luh.*** Wǒ yù dìng le 我 预 定 了 。
My name is _____.	***Wuh jee-aow_____.*** Wǒ jiào 我 叫 _____ 。
How much is a _____.	***_____, dwuh shaow chee-en?*** duō shǎo qián _____ , 多 少 钱 ?

dormitory bed	***dwuh ren fahng chwahng way*** duō rén fáng chuáng wèi 多 人 房 床　位
single room	***dahn ren fahng*** dān rén fáng 单 人 房
standard room	***bee-aow jwun jee-en*** biāo zhǔn jiān 标　准　间
suite	***taow fahng*** tào　fáng 套　房
I want a room _____.	***Wuh yaow ee guh_____ duh fahng jee-en.*** Wǒ　yào yí　gè 我 要 一 个＿＿＿＿ de　fáng jiān 的 房　间 。
with an ocean view	***kuh ee kahn hye*** kě　yǐ　kàn hǎi 可 以 看 海
with a twin-bed	***shwahng ren chwahng*** shuāng rén chuáng 双　　人床
with windows	***dye chwahng who*** dài chuāng hu 带 窗　户

with smoking allowed

kuh ee shee yahn
kě yǐ xī yān
可以吸烟

Can I see the room?

*Wuh nung kahn kahn
fahng jee-en mah?*
Wǒ néng kàn kan fáng jiān ma
我能 看看房 间 吗？

May I have a hotel
name card?

*Yoh liew gwahn duh
ming pee-en mah?*
Yǒu lǚ guǎn de míng piàn ma
有旅馆 的名 片 吗？

May I have an additional
bed in my room?

*Wuh kuh ee jee-ah
ee jahng chwahng mah?*
Wǒ kě yǐ jiā yì zhāng
我可以加一张
chuáng ma
床 吗？

May I change to another
room?

*Wuh kuh ee hwahn guh
fahng jee-en mah?*
Wǒ kě yǐ huàn gè
我可以换 个
fáng jiān ma
房 间 吗？

My room _____.

Wuh duh fahng jee-en ___.
Wǒ de fáng jiān
我的房 间 _____。

has cockroaches

yoh jahng lahng
yǒu zhāng láng
有蟑 螂

has no AC

may yoh kohng tee-aow
méi yǒu kōng tiáo
没 有 空 调

has no hot water

may yoh ruh shway
méi yǒu rè shuǐ
没 有 热 水

is too humid

tye chaow shir luh
tài cháo shī le
太 潮 湿 了

is too noisy

tye chaow luh
tài chǎo le
太 吵 了

has a bad odor

yoh gwye way-ar
yǒu guài wèi er
有 怪 味 儿

Could you bring me ____?

Kuh ee gay wuh ___ mah?
Kě yǐ gěi wǒ   ma
可 以 给 我____吗?

a bar of soap

ee kwyer shee-ahng zaow
yí kuài er xiāng zào
一 块 儿 香 皂

a bed sheet

ee tee-aow chwahng dahn
yì tiáo chuáng dān
一 条 床 单

two blankets

lee-ahng tee-aow tahn zih
liǎng tiáo tǎn zi
两 条 毯 子

a pillow

ee guh jen toh
yí gè zhěn tou
一 个 枕 头

a roll of toilet paper	***ee jwahn way shung jir***
	yì juǎn wèi shēng zhǐ
	一 卷 卫 生 纸

shampoo	***shee fah shee-ahng bwuh***
	xǐ fà xiāng bō
	洗 发 香 波

two towels	***lee-ahng tee-aow***
	maow jee-en
	liǎng tiáo máo jīn
	两 条 毛 巾

I would like a wake-up call.	***Wuh yaow jee-aow shing***
	dee-en hwah.
	Wǒ yào jiào xǐng diàn huà
	我 要 叫 醒 电 话 。

Would you wake me up	***Nee kuh ee _____***
at _____?	***jee-aow shing wuh mah?***
	Nǐ kě yǐ
	你 可 以 _____
	jiào xǐng wǒ ma
	叫 醒 我 吗 ？

4:00 A.M.	***zaow shahng sih dee-en***
	zǎo shang sì diǎn
	早 上 四 点

4:30 A.M.	***zaow shahng sih dee-en bahn***
	zǎo shang sì diǎn bàn
	早 上 四 点 半

5:00 A.M.	***zaow shahng woo dee-en***
	zǎo shang wǔ diǎn
	早 上 五 点

5:30 A.M.	***zaow shahng woo dee-en bahn***
	zǎo shang wǔ diǎn bàn
	早 上 五 点 半

6:00 A.M.	***zaow shahng leo dee-en***
	zǎo shang liù diǎn
	早 上 六 点

6:30 A.M.	***zaow shahng leo dee-en bahn***
	zǎo shang liù diǎn bàn
	早 上 六 点 半

7:00 A.M.	***zaow shahng chee dee-en***
	zǎo shang qī diǎn
	早 上 七 点

7:30 A.M.	***zaow shahng chee dee-en bahn***
	zǎo shang qī diǎn bàn
	早 上 七 点 半

Please clean my room.

***Ching dah saow
wuh duh fahng jee-en.***
Qǐng dǎ sǎo wǒ de fáng jiān
请 打 扫 我 的 房 间 。

Could I have these clothes washed, please?

***Ching bah jay shee-eh
ee foo shee gahn jing,
shee-eh, shee-eh.***
Qǐng bǎ zhè xiē yī fu
请 把 这 些 衣 服
xǐ gān jìng   xiè xie
洗 干 净 ， 谢 谢 。

I would like to check out.

***Wuh shee-ahng
tway fahng.***
Wǒ xiǎng tuì fáng
我 想 退 房 。

May I pay with my credit card?

***Kuh ee yohng
sheen yohng kah mah?***
Kě yǐ yòng xìn yòng kǎ ma
可 以 用 信 用 卡 吗 ？

air conditioning	*kohng tee-aow*	kōng tiáo 空 调
barber shop	*lee fah dee-en*	lǐ fà diàn 理 发 店
clean	*gahn jing*	gān jìng 干 净
fax	*chwahn jen*	chuán zhēn 传 真
heating	*nwahn chee*	nuǎn qì 暖 气
key	*yaow shir*	yào shi 钥 匙
laundry	*shee ee foo*	xǐ yī fu 洗 衣 服
lobby	*dah ting*	dà tīng 大 厅
not clean	*boo gahn jing*	bù gān jìng 不 干 净
telephone	*dee-en hwah*	diàn huà 电 话
television	*dee-en shir*	diàn shì 电 视
toilet	*tsuh swuh*	cè suǒ 厕 所

路遥知马力
日久见人心

Over a long distance, you learn about the strength of your horse. Over a long time, you learn about the character of your friend.

Loo yaow jir mah lee.

Rr jeo jee-en ren sheen.

Divine

Shen

VIII. Food & Drinks

■ Expressions

Waiter / Waitress!	*Foo woo ywahn!* Fú wù yuán 服 务 员 ！
May I see the menu?	*Wuh kuh ee kahn tsye dahn mah?* Wǒ kě yǐ kàn cài dān ma 我 可 以 看 菜 单 吗 ？
May I order now?	*Wuh kuh ee dee-en tsye mah?* Wǒ kě yǐ diǎn cài ma 我 可 以 点 菜 吗 ？
I'm a vegeterian.	*Wuh chir soo.* Wǒ chī sù 我 吃 素 。
I don't eat _____.	*Wuh boo chir _____.* Wǒ bù chī 我 不 吃 _____ 。

duck	*yah roh*	yā ròu 鸭 肉
dog	*goh roh*	gǒu ròu 狗 肉
fish	*yiew*	yú 鱼
turtle	*wahng bah*	wáng ba 王 八
snake	*shuh*	shé 蛇
insects	*chohng zih*	chóng zi 虫 子

Please bring me the bill.	*Wuh mye dahn,*
	shee-eh shee-eh.

Wǒ mǎi dān   xiè xie
我 买 单，谢 谢 。

■ General Words

bread	*mee-en baow*	miàn bāo 面 包
Chinese food	*Johng gwuh tsye*	Zhōng guó cài 中 国 菜
cooked rice	*mee fahn*	mǐ fàn 米 饭
draft beer	*jah pee*	zhā pí 扎 啤
fried rice	*chaow mee fahn*	chǎo mǐ fàn 炒 米 饭
garlic	*swahn*	suàn 蒜
hot (spicy)	*lah duh*	là de 辣 的
menu	*tsye dahn*	cài dān 菜 单
MSG	*way jing*	wèi jīng 味 精
noodles	*mee-en tee-aow*	miàn tiáo 面 条
pepper	*who jee-aow*	hú jiāo 胡 椒
salt	*yahn*	yán 盐
soy sauce	*jee-ahng yoh*	jiàng yóu 酱 油
spicy	*lah (duh)*	là de 辣 （的）
sugar	*tahng*	táng 糖
vinegar	*tsoo*	cù 醋

Could you please
give me _____?

Kuh ee gay wuh
_____ mah?
Kě yǐ gěi wǒ   ma
可 以 给 我 _____ 吗?

a bowl

ee guh wahn
yí gè wǎn
一 个 碗

a cup / glass

ee guh bay zih
yí gè bēi zi
一 个 杯 子

a fork

ee guh chah zih
yí gè chā zi
一 个 叉 子

a knife

ee bah tsahn daow
yì bǎ cān dāo
一 把 餐 刀

some napkins

ee shee-eh tsahn jeen jir
yì xiē cān jīn zhǐ
一 些 餐 巾 纸

a pair of chopsticks

ee shwahng kwye zih
yì shuāng kuài zi
一 双   筷 子

a plate

ee guh pahn zih
yí gè pán zi
一 个 盘 子

a spoon

ee guh shaow zih
yí gè sháo zi
一 个 勺 子

■ Drinks

Please give me a beer.	***Ching gay wuh ee guh pee jeo.***	
	Qǐng gěi wǒ yí gè pí jiǔ	
	请 给 我 一 个 啤 酒 。	

A cold one.	***Yaow bing duh.***	
	Yào bīng de	
	要 冰 的 。	

With ice, please.	***Yaow jee-ah bing.***	
	Yào jiā bīng	
	要 加 冰 。	

I would like a cup / glass of ___.	***Wuh yaow ee bay _____.***	
	Wǒ yào yì bēi	
	我 要 一 杯 _____ 。	

apple juice	***ping gwuh jir***	píng guǒ zhī 苹 果 汁
beer	***pee jeo***	pí jiǔ 啤 酒
coffee	***kah fay***	kā fēi 咖 啡
draft beer	***jah pee***	zhā pí 扎 啤
juice (fruit)	***gwuh jir***	guǒ zhī 果 汁
lemonade	***ning mung shway***	níng méng shuǐ 柠 檬 水
milk	***niew nye***	niú nǎi 牛 奶
orange juice	***chung jir***	chéng zhī 橙 汁
tea	***chah***	chá 茶

tomato juice	*shee hohng shir jir*	xī hóng shì zhī 西 红 柿 汁
Tsingtao beer	*Ching daow pee jeo*	Qīng dǎo pí jiǔ 青 岛 啤 酒
water	*shway*	shuǐ 水
whisky	*way shir jee*	wēi shì jì 威 士 忌
wine	*poo taow jeo*	pú tao jiǔ 葡 萄 酒

■ Fruit

I would like a fruit salad.	***Wuh yaow ee guh shway gwuh shah lah.***	Wǒ yào yí gè shuǐ guǒ shā la 我 要 一 个 水 果 沙 拉。
I would like a couple of _____.	***Wuh yaow lee-ahng guh _____.***	Wǒ yào liǎng gè 我 要 两 个 _____。

apples	*ping gwuh*	píng guǒ 苹 果
apricots	*shing*	xìng 杏
bananas	*shee-ahng jee-aow*	xiāng jiāo 香 蕉
dates	*zaow*	zǎo 枣
fruit	*shway gwuh*	shuǐ guǒ 水 果
grapes	*poo taow*	pú tao 葡 萄
mango	*mahng gwuh*	máng guǒ 芒 果

muskmelon	*hah mee gwah*	hā mì guā 哈密瓜
oranges	*jiew zih*	jú zi 橘子
papaya	*moo gwah*	mù guā 木瓜
peaches	*taow zih*	táo zi 桃子
pears	*lee*	lí 梨
pineapples	*buh lwuh*	bō luó 菠萝
plums	*lee zih*	lǐ zi 李子
strawberries	*tsaow may*	cǎo méi 草莓
tangerines	*gahn jiew*	gān jú 柑橘
watermelon	*shee gwah*	xī guā 西瓜

■ Soup

I would like a _____.   *Wuh yaow ee guh _____.*
Wǒ yào yí gè
我要一个 _____。

beef soup cooked with
Chinese watermelon
neo roh dohng gwah
tahng
niú ròu dōng guā tāng
牛肉冬瓜汤

chicken soup cooked with
mushroom
jee roh mwuh goo
tahng
jī ròu mó gu tāng
鸡肉蘑菇汤

89

fish soup

yiew tahng
yú tāng
鱼 汤

pork soup cooked with
Sichuan pickles

*jah tsye roh sih
tahng*
zhà cài ròu sī tāng
榨 菜 肉 丝 汤

spicy and sour soup

swahn lah tahng
suān là tāng
酸 辣 汤

tomato and egg soup

*shee hohng shir jee dahn
tahng*
xī hóng shì jī dàn tāng
西 红 柿 鸡 蛋 汤

vegetable soup

shoo tsye tahng
shū cài tāng
蔬 菜 汤

■ Vegetable Dishes

I would like a _____.

Wuh yaow ee guh _____.
Wǒ yào yí gè
我 要 一 个 _____。

bamboo shoots, plain fried

ching chaow swun peer
qīng chǎo sǔn piàn
清 炒 笋 片

bean curds, family style

jee-ah chahng doh foo
jiā cháng dòu fu
家 常 豆 腐

spicy bean curds	**mah lah doh foo** má là dòu fu 麻 辣 豆 腐
broccoli, garlic flavored	**swahn rohng shee lahn hwah** suàn róng xī lán huā 蒜 蓉 西 兰 花
broccoli, plain fried	**ching chaow shee lahn hwah** qīng chǎo xī lán huā 清 炒 西 兰 花
cabbage, vinegar flavored	**tsoo leo bye tsye** cù liū bái cài 醋 溜 白 菜
celery, fried with cashew nuts	**yaow gwuh shee cheen** yāo guǒ xī qín 腰 果 西 芹
celery, fried with lily petal	**shee cheen bye huh** xī qín bǎi hé 西 芹 百 合
eggplant, fried with peppers and potatoes	**dee sahn shee-en** dì sān xiān 地 三 鲜
eggplant, spicy with garlic	**yiew shee-ahng chee-eh zih** yú xiāng qié zi 鱼 香 茄 子
Holland beans, garlic flavored	**swahn rohng huh lahn doh** suàn róng hé lán dòu 蒜 蓉 荷 兰 豆

mixed vegetables	***soo shir jeen*** sù shí jīn 素 什 锦
peanuts, deep fried, salty flavored	***yoh jah hwah shung*** ***mee*** yóu zhá huā shēng mǐ 油 炸 花 生 米
shredded potatoes, vinegar flavored	***tsoo leo too doh sih*** cù liū tǔ dòu sī 醋 溜 土 豆 丝
spinach, garlic flavored	***swahn rohng bwuh tsye*** suàn róng bō cài 蒜 蓉 菠 菜
string beans, garlic flavored	***swahn rohng doh*** ***jee-aow*** suàn róng dòu jiǎo 蒜 蓉 豆 角
string beans, sautéed	***gahn bee-en doh jee-aow*** gān biān dòu jiǎo 干 煸 豆 角
tomatoes, fried with eggs	***jee dahn chaow*** ***shee hohng shir*** jī dàn chǎo xī hóng shì 鸡 蛋 炒 西 红 柿
asparagus	***loo swun***	lú sǔn 芦 笋
bamboo shoots	***joo swun***	zhú sǔn 竹 笋
bean curds	***doh foo***	dòu fu 豆 腐
bean sprouts	***doh yah***	dòu yá 豆 芽

beans	*doh zih*	dòu zi 豆子
broccoli	*yee-eh tsye*	yē cài 椰菜
cabbage	*bye tsye*	bái cài 白菜
carrots	*hoo lwuh bwuh*	hú luó bo 胡萝卜
celery	*cheen tsye*	qín cài 芹菜
chili	*lah jee-aow*	là jiāo 辣椒
cucumber	*hwahng gwah*	huáng guā 黄瓜
eggplant	*chee-eh zih*	qié zi 茄子
garlic	*swahn*	suàn 蒜
ginger	*jee-ahng*	jiāng 姜
green onions	*tsohng*	cōng 葱
green peppers	*ching jee-aow*	qīng jiāo 青椒
kidney beans	*yaow doh*	yāo dòu 腰豆
lettuce	*shung tsye*	shēng cài 生菜
mushrooms	*mwuh goo*	mó gu 蘑菇
peanuts	*hwah shung*	huā shēng 花生
peas	*wahn doh*	wān dòu 豌豆
potatoes	*too doh*	tǔ dòu 土豆
spinach	*bwuh tsye*	bō cài 菠菜

string beans   ***sih jee doh***

sì jì dòu
四 季 豆

tomatoes   ***shee hohng shir***

xī hóng shì
西 红 柿

■ Meat Dishes

I would like _____.   ***Wuh yaow ee guh*** _____.

Wǒ yào yí gè
我 要 一 个   _____ 。

beef, black pepper flavored   ***hay jee-aow neo leo***

hēi jiāo niú liǔ
黑 椒 牛 柳

beef, braised   ***hohng men neo roh***

hóng mèn niú ròu
红 焖 牛 肉

beef, fried & served on
a hot iron plate   ***tee-eh bahn neo leo***

tiě bǎn niú liǔ
铁 板 牛 柳

beef, fried with
green pepper   ***neo roh chaow
ching jee-aow***

niú ròu chǎo qīng jiāo
牛 肉 炒 青 椒

chicken wings, braised   ***hohng men jee chir***

hóng mèn jī chì
红 焖 鸡 翅

chicken, fried with peanuts,
spicy flavored   ***gohng baow jee ding***

gōng bào jī dīng
宫 爆 鸡 丁

chicken, lemon flavored

ning mung jee
níng méng jī
柠 檬 鸡

chicken, shredded,
spicy flavored

yiew shee-ahng jee sih
yú xiāng jī sī
鱼 香 鸡 丝

chicken, sweet and sour

tahng tsoo jee pee-en
táng cù jī piàn
糖 醋 鸡 片

crab

pahng shee-eh
páng xiè
螃 蟹

fish, sweet and sour

tahng tsoo yiew pee-en
táng cù yú piàn
糖 醋 鱼 片

lamb kabob

yahng roh chwahn
yáng ròu chuàn
羊 肉 串

lobster

lohng shee-ah
lóng xiā
龙 虾

pork, sweet and sour

tahng tsoo lee jee
táng cù lǐ ji
糖 醋 里 脊

prawn, sweet and sour

tahng tsoo shee-ah
táng cù xiā
糖 醋 虾

beef	*neo roh*	niú ròu 牛 肉
chicken	*jee roh*	jī ròu 鸡 肉
crab	*pahng shee-eh*	páng xiè 螃 蟹
duck	*yah roh*	yā ròu 鸭 肉
fish	*yiew*	yú 鱼
lamb	*yahng roh*	yáng ròu 羊 肉
lobster	*lohng shee-ah*	lóng xiā 龙 虾
mutton	*yahng roh*	yáng ròu 羊 肉
oysters	*moo lee*	mǔ lì 牡 蛎
pigeon	*guh zih*	gē zi 鸽 子
pork	*joo roh*	zhū ròu 猪 肉
salmon	*sahn wen yiew*	sān wén yú 三 文 鱼
shark's fin	*yiew chir*	yú chì 鱼 翅
shrimp	*shee-ah*	xiā 虾
steak	*niew pye*	niú pái 牛 排
rare	*bahn shoh duh*	bàn shú de 半 熟 的
medium	*chee fen shoh duh*	qī fēn shú de 七 分 熟 的
well done	*chwahn shoh duh*	quán shú de 全 熟 的

民以食为天

Food is god.
Meen ee shir way tee-en.

Happiness

Shee

IX. Shopping

▼ Don't forget to ask for a discount while shopping in China!

Where can I buy_____?

Wuh zye nahr kuh ee mye _____?
Wǒ zài nǎ ér kě yǐ mǎi
我 在 哪 儿 可 以 买 ____ ?

art supplies

may shoo yohng peen
měi shù yòng pǐn
美 术 用 品

bedding

chwahng shahng yohng peen
chuáng shàng yòng pǐn
床 上 用 品

childrens clothing

ar tohng foo jwahng
ér tóng fú zhuāng
儿 童 服 装

computer equipment

jee swahn jee pay jee-en
jì suàn jī pèi jiàn
计 算 机 配 件

DVDs

DVD

flowers

shee-en hwah
xiān huā
鲜 花

groceries

rr yohng peen
rì yòng pǐn
日 用 品

jewelry	***shoh shir*** shǒu shì 首 饰
men's clothing	***nahn shir foo jwahng*** nán shì fú zhuāng 男 士 服 装
office supplies	***bahn gohng yohng peen*** bàn gōng yòng pǐn 办 公 用 品
plants	***jir woo*** zhí wù 植 物
sports equipment	***tee yiew yohng peen*** tǐ yù yòng pǐn 体 育 用 品
sunglasses	***tye yahng jing*** tài yáng jìng 太 阳 镜
a watch	***shoh bee-aow*** shǒu biǎo 手 表
women's clothing	***niew shir foo jwahng*** nǚ shì fú zhuāng 女 士 服 装

I would like to buy _____.	***Wuh shee-ahng mye ____.*** Wǒ xiǎng mǎi 我 想 买 _____ 。

How much does it cost?

Dwuh shaow chee-en?
Duō shǎo qián
多 少 钱 ?

It's too expensive!

Tye gway lah!
Tài guì la
太 贵 啦 !

Any discount?

Dah juh mah?
Dǎ zhé ma
打 折 吗 ?

May I try it on?

Wuh kuh ee shir shir mah?
Wǒ kě yǐ shì shi ma
我 可 以 试 试 吗 ?

Sorry, I don't like it.

Dway boo chee,
wuh boo shee hwahn.
Duì bu qǐ   wǒ bù xǐ huān
对 不 起，我 不 喜 欢 。

■ Color

I don't like this color.

Wuh boo shee hwahn
jay guh yahn suh.
Wǒ bù xǐ huan zhè ge yán sè
我 不 喜 欢 这 个 颜 色。

Are there other colors
of this?

Yoh bee-eh duh
yahn suh mah?
Yǒu bié de yán sè ma
有 别 的 颜 色 吗 ?

Do you have a ____ one? **Yoh _____ mah?**
Yǒu   ma
有 _____ 吗 ?

black	*hay duh*	hēi de 黑 的
blue	*lahn duh*	lán de 蓝 的
brown	*zohng suh duh*	zōng sè de 棕 色 的
darker	*gung shen duh*	gèng shēn de 更 深 的
gray	*hway duh*	huī de 灰 的
green	*liew duh*	lǜ de 绿 的
lighter	*gung chee-en duh*	gèng qiǎn de 更 浅 的
orange	*jiew hohng duh*	jú hóng de 桔 红 的
pink	*fen duh*	fěn de 粉 的
purple	*zih suh duh*	zǐ sè de 紫 色 的
red	*hohng duh*	hóng de 红 的
white	*bye duh*	bái de 白 的
yellow	*hwahng duh*	huáng de 黄 的

■ Size

Do you have a _____ one? **Yoh _____ mah?**

Yǒu   ma

有 _____ 吗 ?

bigger	*gung dah duh*	gèng dà de 更 大 的
longer	*gung chahng duh*	gèng cháng de 更 长 的
shorter	*gung dwahn duh*	gèng duǎn de 更 短 的
smaller	*gung shee-aow duh*	gèng xiǎo de 更 小 的

不入虎穴

焉得虎子

Nothing ventured, nothing gained.
Boo roo hoo shweh, yahn duh hoo zih.

Trust
Sheen

X. Bank & Postal

■ Bank

I would like to wire my money to this address.	***Wuh shee-ahng bah chee-en hway daow jay guh dee jir.***

Wǒ xiǎng bǎ qián
我 想 把 钱

huì dào zhè ge dì zhǐ
汇 到 这 个 地 址 。

I would like to deposit some money.	***Wuh shee-ahng tswun chee-en.***

Wǒ xiǎng cùn qián
我 想 存 钱 。

I would like to withdraw some money.	***Wuh shee-ahng chiew chee-en.***

Wǒ xiǎng qǔ qián
我 想 取 钱 。

I would like to have them in _____.	***Wuh shee-ahng yaow_____.***

Wǒ xiǎng yào
我 想 要 _____。

RMB	***Ren meen bee***	Rén mín bì 人 民 币
USD	***May ywahn***	Měi yuán 美 元
Euros	***Oh ywahn***	Ou yuán 欧 元

I would like to withdraw
money from this
credit card.

*Wuh shee-ahng tsohng
jay jahng kah lee
chiew chee-en.*

Wǒ xiǎng cóng zhè zhāng
我 想 从 这 张
kǎ lǐ qǔ qián
卡 里 取 钱 。

What's the
commission fee?

*Shoh shiew fay shir
dwuh shaow?*

Shǒu xù fèi shì duō shǎo
手 续 费 是 多 少 ？

I would like to pay
my mobile phone.

*Wuh shee-ahng gay
shoh jee jee-aow fay.*

Wǒ xiǎng gěi shǒu jī jiāo fèi
我 想 给 手 机 交 费。

My bank card
was swallowed
by the ATM machine!

*Wuh duh kah
bay chiew kwahn jee
chir dee-aow luh!*

Wǒ de kǎ bèi qǔ kuǎn jī
我 的 卡 被 取 款 机
chī diào le
吃 掉 了 ！

ATM machine	*zih dohng*	zì dòng 自 动
	chiew kwahn jee	qǔ kuǎn jī 取 款 机
bank	*yeen hahng*	yín háng 银 行
deposit	*tswun kwahn*	cún kuǎn 存 款
wire money	*hway kwahn*	huì kuǎn 汇 款
withdraw	*chiew chee-en*	qǔ qián 取 钱

■ Post Office

May I have _____?	**Kuh-ee gay wuh ____ mah?**
	Kě yǐ gěi wǒ ma
	可 以 给 我 _____ 吗 ？

an envelope

ee guh sheen fung
yí gè xìn fēng
一 个 信 封

an international envelope

ee guh gwuh jee sheen fung
yí gè guó jì xìn fēng
一 个 国 际 信 封

a postage stamp

ee jahng yoh pee-aow
yì zhāng yóu piào
一 张 邮 票

a postcard

ee jahng ming sheen pee-en
yì zhāng míng xìn piàn
一 张 明 信 片

a packing box

ee guh huh zih
yí gè hé zi
一 个 盒 子

I would like to mail this to _____.

Wuh shee-ahng bah jay guh jee daow _____.
Wǒ xiǎng bǎ
我 想 把
zhè ge jì dào
这 个 寄 到 _____。

America   **May gwuh**
Měi guó
美 国

Australia	***Aow dah lee yah***	Ao dà lì yà 澳 大 利 亚
Canada	***Jee-ah nah dah***	Jiā ná dà 加 拿 大
England	***Ying gwuh***	Yīng guó 英 国
New Zealand	***Sheen shee lahn***	Xīn xī lán 新 西 兰

I would like to mail it _____.   ***Wuh jee _____.***

Wǒ jì
我 寄_____。

as air mail	***hahng kohng yoh jee-en*** háng kōng yóu jiàn 航 空 邮 件
as express mail	***tuh kwye jwahn dee*** tè kuài zhuān dì 特 快 专 递
as ordinary mail	***poo tohng yoh jee-en*** pǔ tōng yóu jiàn 普 通 邮 件
as registered mail	***gwah haow shee-en*** guà hào xìn 挂 号 信
the cheapest way	***zway pee-en ee duh*** zuì pián yi de 最 便 宜 的
the fastest way	***zway kwye duh*** zuì kuài de 最 快 的

How much does it cost?	***Dwuh shaow chee-en?*** Duō shǎo qián 多 少 钱 ？
I'm here to collect my package.	***Wuh lye chiew baow gwuh.*** Wǒ lái qù bāo guǒ 我 来 取 包 裹 。
Here is my passport.	***Juh shir wuh duh*** ***hoo jaow.*** Zhè shì wǒ de hù zhào 这 是 我 的 护 照 。
Here is my receipt.	***Juh shir wuh duh*** ***baow gwuh dahn.*** Zhè shì wǒ de bāo guǒ dān 这 是 我 的 包 裹 单 。

■ Telecommunications

Where can I _____?	***Wuh zye nar kuh ee ____?*** Wǒ zài nǎ er kě yǐ 我 在 哪 儿 可 以 ____ ？
get online	***shahng wahng*** shàng wǎng 上 网
make a collect call	***dah dway fahng*** ***foo kwahn dee-en hwah*** dǎ duì fāng fù kuǎn diàn huà 打 对 方 付 款 电 话
make a direct-dial call	***dah jir bwuh dee-en hwah*** dǎ zhí bō diàn huà 打 直 拨 电 话

make an international call	**dah gwuh jee chahng too**	dǎ guó jì cháng tú 打 国 际 长 途
send a fax	**fah chwahn jen**	fā chuán zhēn 发 传 真
receive a fax	**shoh chwahn jen**	shōu chuán zhēn 收 传 真
email	**dee-en zih** **yoh jee-en**	diàn zǐ 电 子 yóu jiàn 邮 件
envelope	**sheen fung**	xìn fēng 信 封
fax	**chwahn jen**	chuán zhēn 传 真
international call	**gwuh jee dee-en hwah**	guó jì diàn huà 国 际 电 话
internet	**yeen tuh wahng**	yīn tè wǎng 因 特 网
online	**shahng wahng**	shàng wǎng 上 网
package	**baow gwuh**	bāo guǒ 包 裹
postage stamp	**yoh pee-aow**	yóu piào 邮 票
to collect a package	**chiew baow gwuh**	qǔ bāo guǒ 取 包 裹
to collect	**chiew**	qǔ 取
to mail	**jee**	jì 寄

to mail a letter   *jee sheen*   jì xìn 寄信

to mail a package   *jee baow gwuh*   jì bāo guǒ 寄包裹

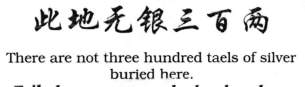

此地无银三百两

There are not three hundred taels of silver buried here.
Tsih dee woo yeen sahn bye lee-ahng.

Moral: A nervous person is prone to make mistakes; overkill will worsen a situation.

The story: A man buried his three hundred taels of silver, and not wanting others to find it, he put a sign above it saying: There are not three hundred taels of silver buried here. Overnight, his neighbor, Ah-er stole the silver. Not wanting to draw suspicion to himself, Ah-er put another sign there stating: Your neighbor Ah-er did not steal them.

Blessing

Foo

XI. Health & Emergencies

I, He / She _____.

Wuh,Tah _____.
Wǒ   Tā   Tā
我，他/她 _____。

am / is Injured
shoh shahng luh
shòu shāng le
受 伤 了

caught a cold
gahn maow luh
gǎn mào le
感 冒 了

vomited
too luh
tù le
吐 了

have / has diarrhea
zye lah doo zih
zài lā dù zi
在 拉 肚 子

am / is having
a headache
toh tung
tóu téng
头 疼

am / is sick
bing luh
bìng le
病 了

She needs to go to
the hospital.
**Tah shiew yaow chiew
ee ywahn.**
Tā xū yào qù yī yuàn
她 需 要 去 医 院 。

Please call an ambulance.
Ching jaow jiew hoo chuh.
Qǐng jiào jiù hù chē
请 叫 救 护 车 。

Please call the police.	***Ching jee-aow jing chah.***
	Qǐng jiào jǐng chá
	请 叫 警 察 。

		shāng fēng
a cold	***shahng fung***	伤 风
		zhēn jiǔ
acupuncture	***jen jeo***	针 灸
		jiù hù chē
ambulance	***jeo hoo chuh***	救 护 车
		A sī pǐ lín
Aspirin	***Ah sih pee leen***	阿 斯 匹 林
		xiào chuǎn
asthma	***shee-aow chwahn***	哮 喘
		liú xuè
bleeding	***leo shweh***	流 血
		xīn jiǎo tòng
chest cramp	***sheen jee-aow tohng***	心 绞 痛
		shāng fēng
cold	***shahng fung***	伤 风
		biàn mì
constipation	***bee-en mee***	便 秘
		ké sou
cough	***kuh soh***	咳 嗽
		yá yī
dentist	***yah ee***	牙 医
		lā dù zi
diarrhea	***lah doo zih***	拉 肚 子
		tóu yūn
dizzy	***toh ywin***	头 晕
		yī shēng
doctor	***ee-shung*** or	医 生 ；
		dài fu
	dye foo	大 夫
		yào diàn
drugstore	***yaow dee-en***	药 店
		jiǎn chá
examination	***jee-en chah***	检 查

fever	*fah shaow*	fā shāo 发 烧
flu	*gahn maow*	gǎn mào 感 冒
flu medications	*gahn maow yaow*	gǎn mào yào 感 冒 药
headache	*toh tung*	tóu téng 头 疼
health insurance	*ee lee-aow*	yī liáo 医 疗
	baow shee-en	hǎo xiǎn 保 险
high blood pressure	*gaow shweh yah*	gāo xuè yā 高 血 压
hospital	*ee ywahn*	yī yuàn 医 院
infection	*gahn rahn*	gǎn rǎn 感 染
injection	*dah jen*	dǎ zhēn 打 针
injured	*shoh shahng luh*	shòu shāngle 受 伤 了
massage	*ahn mwuh*	àn mó 按 摩
medicine	*yaow*	yào 药
operation	*shoh shoo*	shǒu shù 手 术
pain	*tung*	téng 疼
pill	*yaow pee-en*	yào piàn 药 片
pneumonia	*fay yahn*	fèi yán 肺 炎
prescription	*yaow fahng*	yào fāng 药 方
sick	*bing luh*	bìng le 病 了

sore throat	**sahng zih tung**	sǎng zi téng 嗓 子 疼
stomachache	**way tung**	wèi téng 胃 疼
toothache	**yah tung**	yá téng 牙 疼
vomit	**oh too**	ǒu tù 呕 吐
X-ray	**X gwahng**	guāng X 光
pain relievers	**chiew tohng pee-en**	qù tòng piàn 去 痛 片
vitamins	**way tah ming**	wéi tā mìng 维 他 命
Vitamin C	**Way tah ming C**	Wéi tā mìng 维 他 命 C

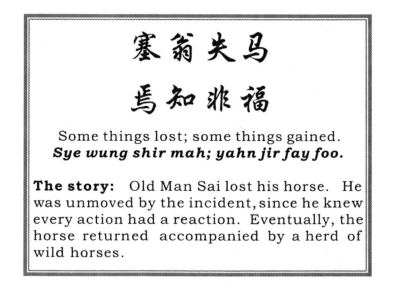

塞翁失马
焉知非福

Some things lost; some things gained.
Sye wung shir mah; yahn jir fay foo.

The story: Old Man Sai lost his horse. He was unmoved by the incident, since he knew every action had a reaction. Eventually, the horse returned accompanied by a herd of wild horses.

Love
Eye

Travelling with Infants

His / Her name is _____. **Tah jee-aow _____.**
Tā   Tā jiào
他 / 她叫 _____。

He / She is _____   **Tah _____ guh**
months old.   **yiew dah.**
Tā   Tā   gè yuè dà
他 / 她_____个 月 大 。

He / She is ____ years old. **Tah _____ sway.**
Tā   Tā   suì
他 / 她_____岁 。

one	*ee*	yí 一	eight	*bah*	bā 八
two	*lee-ahng*	liǎng 两	nine	*jeo*	jiǔ 九
three	*sahn*	sān 三	ten	*shir*	shí 十
four	*sih*	sì 四	eleven	*shir ee*	shí yī 十一
five	*woo*	wǔ 五	twelve	*shir ar*	shí èr 十二
six	*leo*	liù 六	thirteen	*shir sahn*	shí sān 十三
seven	*chee*	qī 七	fourteen	*shir sih*	shí sì 十四

Where can I find _____? **Nah lee yoh _____?**
Nǎ lǐ yǒu
哪 里 有_____?

baby clothes   **ying ar ee foo**
yīng ér yī fu
婴 儿 衣 服

baby food

ying ar shir peen
yīng ér shí pǐn
婴 儿 食 品

baby supplies

ying ar yohng peen
yīng ér yòng pǐn
婴 儿 用 品

children's Tylenol

ar tohng jir tung pee-en
ér tóng zhǐ téng piàn
儿 童 止 疼 片

diapers

nee-aow boo shir
niào bù shī
尿 不 湿

an international clinic

gwuh jee jen swuh
guó jì zhěn suǒ
国 际 诊 所

a pediatrician

ar kuh ee shung
ér kē yī shēng
儿 科 医 生

He / She is coughing
too much.

**Tah kuh soh duh
hen lee hye.**
Tā   Tā ké sou de hěn lì hài
他 / 她咳嗽 得 很 厉 害。

He / She is crying a lot.

**Tah koo duh
hen lee hye.**
Tā   Tā kū de hěn lì hài
他 / 她哭得很 厉 害。

He / She is sick.

Tah bing luh.
Tā   Tā bìng le
他 / 她病 了。

He / She isn't sleeping at night.

Tah wahn shahng boo shway jee-aow.

Tā Tā wǎn shang bú shuì jiào
他／她晚上 不睡觉。

He / She is vomiting.

Tah zohng shir too.

Tā Tā zǒng shì tù
他／她总 是吐。

He / She has diarrhea.

Tah lah doo zih luh.

Tā Tā lā dù zi le
他／她拉肚子了。

He / She has a fever.

Tah zye fah shaow.

Tā Tā zài fā shāo
他／她在发烧。

He / She will not eat.

Tah boo chir dohng shee.

Tā Tā bù chī dōng xi
他／她不吃东西。

Can we get _____?

Kuh ee gay wuh men _____ mah?

Kě yǐ gěi wǒ men ma
可以给我们 ___吗？

a crib

ee jahng ying ar chwahng

yì zhāng yīng ér chuáng
一张 婴儿床

a baby blanket

ee kwar ying ar tahn zih

yí kuài er yīng ér tǎn zi
一块儿婴儿毯子

extra towels

lee-ahng kwar maow jeen

liǎng kuài er máo jīn
两 块儿毛巾

Do you have baby food?

Yoh ying ar shir peen mah?
Yǒu yīng ér shí pǐn ma
有 婴 儿 食 品 吗？

Do you have
sanitized wet towels?

Yoh shir jir jeen mah?
Yǒu shī zhǐ jīn ma
有 湿 纸 巾 吗？

Would you please
take our picture?

*Kuh ee gay wuh men jaow
jahng shee-ahng mah?*
Kě yǐ gěi wǒ men zhào
可 以 给 我 们 照
zhāng xiàng ma
张 像 吗？

Can you make room
for my baby and us?

*Kuh ee gay wuh men
rahng ee rahng mah?*
Kě yǐ gěi wǒ men
可 以 给 我 们
ràng yí ràng ma
让 一 让 吗？

Where can I
change my baby?

*Wuh kuh ee zye nahr
gay hye zih hwahn
nee-aow boo?*
Wǒ kě yǐ zài nǎ er
我 可 以 在 哪 儿
gěi hái zi huàn niào bù
给 孩 子 换 尿 布？

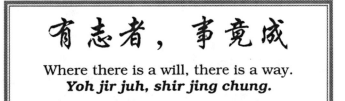

有志者，事竟成

Where there is a will, there is a way.
Yoh jir juh, shir jing chung.

Propriety
Lee

XIII. Go Ahead and Say It

In Alphabetical Order (Mostly)

Are you crazy?

Nee fung luh mah?
Nǐ fēng le ma
你 疯 了 吗？

Are you serious?

Nee shir ren jen duh mah?
Nǐ shì ròn zhēn de ma
你 是 认 真 的 吗？

Beauty is in the eyes of the beholder.

Ching ren yahn lee choo shee shir.
Qíng rén yǎn lǐ chū xī shī
情 人 眼 里 出 西 施。

Do you love me?

Nee eye wuh mah?
Nǐ ài wǒ ma
你 爱 我 吗？

Of course, I do.

Wuh dahng rahn eye nee.
Wǒ dāng rán ài nǐ
我 当 然 爱 你。

How much do you love me?

Nee yoh dwuh eye wuh?
Nǐ yǒu duō ài wǒ
你 有 多 爱 我？

I love you higher than the mountain, deeper than the sea.

Wuh eye nee bee shahn gaow, bee hye shen.
Wǒ ài nǐ bǐ shān gāo
我 爱 你 比 山 高，
bǐ hǎi shēn
比 海 深。

Do you have condoms?

Nee yoh bee ywin taow mah?
Nǐ yǒu bì yùn tào ma
你 有 避 孕 套 吗 ？

Everything is fine.

May shir.
Méi shì
没 事 。

Excuse me, I farted.

Dway boo chee, wuh fahng pee luh.
Duì bu qǐ
对 不 起 ，
wǒ fàng pì le
我 放 屁 了 。

Excuse me,
I'm afraid I'm drunk.

Dway boo chee, wuh huh dwuh luh.
Duì bu qǐ   wǒ hē duō le
对 不 起 ，我 喝 多 了 。

Figure it out!

Shee-ahng bahn fah!
Xiǎng bàn fǎ
想   办 法 ！

Have you eaten yet?

Chir luh mah?
Chī le ma
吃 了 吗 ？

He is 250.
(He is an idiot.)

Tah shir ar bye woo.
Tā shì èr bǎi wǔ
他 是 二 百 五 。

He is odd.

Tah jen shee-eh mer.
Tā zhēn xié mén ér
他 真 邪 门 儿 。

He/She is a phony.

Tah hen shiew way.
Tā   Tā hěn xū wěi
他 / 她 很 虚 伪 。

He/She is an idiot.

Tah shir guh bye chir.
Tā   Tā shì gè bái chī
他 / 她 是 个 白 痴 。

How pitiful.

Jen kuh shee.
Zhēn kě xī
真 可 惜 。

I'm horny.

Wuh shee-ahng zwuh eye.
Wǒ xiǎng zuò ài
我 想 做 爱 。

I'm confused.

Wuh bay gaow hoo too luh.
Wǒ bèi gǎo hú tu le
我 被 搞 糊 涂 了 。

I'm kidding.

Wuh kye wahn shee-aow.
Wǒ kāi wán xiào
我 开 玩 笑 。

I'm pissed off.

Wuh hen shung chee.
Wǒ hěn shēng qì
我 很 生 气 。

I'm stressed out.

Wuh fahn sih luh.
Wǒ fán sǐ le
我 烦 死 了 。

I'm stuffed!

Chung sih wuh luh.
Chēng sǐ wǒ le
撑 死 我 了 。

I don't care.

Wuh boo zye hoo.
Wǒ bú zài hu
我 不 在 乎 。

I don't give a shit.

Wuh tah mah duh boo zye hoo.

Wǒ tā mā de bú zài hu

我 他 妈 的 不 在 乎 。

I don't trust you.

Wuh boo shee-ahng sheen nee.

Wǒ bù xiāng xìn nǐ

我 不 相 信 你 。

I screwed up.

Wuh gaow zah luh.

Wǒ gǎo zá le

我 搞 砸 了 。

Is that alright?

Haow boo haow?

Hǎo bù hǎo

好 不 好 ？

It smells like shit.

Wen juh shee-ahng dah bee-en.

Wén zhe xiàng dà biàn

闻 着 象 大 便 。

It tastes like shit.

Nahn chir sih luh.

Nán chī sǐ le

难 吃 死 了 。

It's bullshit.

Chuh dahn.

Chě dàn

扯 淡 。

It's my pleasure.

Boo kuh chee.

Bú kè qi

不 客 气 。

I want to make love to you.
Wuh shee-ahng gen nee zwuh eye.
Wǒ xiǎng gēn nǐ zuò ài
我 想 跟 你 做 爱 。

Let me think about it.
Rahng wuh shee-ahng shee-ahng.
Ràng wǒ xiǎng xiang
让 我 想 想 。

May I ask you to dance?
Wuh kuh oc ching nee tee-aow woo mah?
Wǒ kě yǐ qǐng nǐ tiào wǔ ma
我 可以 请 你 跳 舞 吗?

Nice ass.
Pee-aow lee-ahng duh pee goo.
Piào liang de pì gu
漂 亮 的 屁 股 。

Nonsense.
Hoo shwuh
Hú shuō
胡 说 。

Please wait for your turn!
Ching pye dway.
Qǐng pái duì
请 排队 !

See you soon.
Hway jee-en.
Huí jiàn
回 见 。

It's so embarrassing.
Tye boo haow ee sih luh.
Tài bù hǎo yì si le
太 不 好 意 思 了 。

Sorry, wrong number.

***Dway boo chee,
dah tswuh luh.***

Duì bu qǐ   dǎ cuò le
对 不 起 ， 打 错 了 。

This is total bullshit.

***Juh chwahn shir chuh
dahn.***

Zhè quán shì chě dàn
这 全 是 扯 淡 。

Thank you.
(in Chinese tradition)

***Gwuh jee-ahng,
gwuh jee-ahng.***

Guò jiǎng   guò jiǎng
过 讲 ， 过 讲 。
(Overpraised, overpraised.)
or
Nah lee, Nah lee.

Nǎ li   nǎ li
哪 里 ， 哪 里 。
(Where, where.)

There is nothing we can do.

May bahn fah.

Méi bàn fǎ
没 办 法 。

Well done, comrade.

Gahn duh haow, tohng jir!

Gàn de hǎo   tóng zhì
干 得 好 ， 同 志 ！

What are you doing?

Nee zye gahn shen muh?

Nǐ zài gàn shén me
你 在 干 什 么 ？

▲ **Note:** *gahn* literally means "do". ***Nee shee-ahng
gahn shen muh?*** Literally says: You want to do
what?

▲ **Word of caution:** *Gahn* is also slang for "fuck."

What can we do?

Zen muh bahn?
Zěn me bàn
怎 么 办 ？

What's the matter?

Zen muh luh?
Zěn me le
怎 么 了 ？

Who cares.

Shay zye hoo.
Shuí zài hu
谁 在 乎 。

Who knows.

Tee-en jir daow.
Tiān zhī dào
天 知 道 。

You're a moron.

Nee jen rwuh jir.
Nǐ zhēn ruò zhì
你 真 弱 智 。

You're hopeless.

Nee may jeo lah.
Nǐ méi jiù la
你 没 救 啦 。

You're psycho.

Nee shir shen jing bing.
Nǐ shì shén jīng bìng
你 是 神 精 病 。

You look like shit.

Nee lee-en suh
jen nahn kahn.
Nǐ liǎn sè zhēn nán kàn
你 脸 色 真 难 看 。

You're cute.

Nee jen kuh eye.
Nǐ zhēn kě ài
你 真 可 爱 。

You're so sexy.

Nee jen shing gahn.
Nǐ zhēn xìng gǎn
你 真 性 感 。

You're very clever.

Nee hen tsohng ming.
Nǐ hěn cōng míng
你 很 聪 明 。

You drive me crazy.

Nee rahng wuh fah fung.
Nǐ ràng wǒ fā fēng
你 让 我 发 疯 。

You have beautiful eyes.

**Nee duh yahn jing
jen pee-aow lee-ahng.**
Nǐ de yǎn jīng
你 的 眼 睛
zhēn piào liang
真 漂 亮 。

You fool.

Nee juh shah gwah.
Nǐ zhè shǎ guā
你 这 傻 瓜 。

You scared me.

Shee-ah wuh ee tee-aow.
Xià wǒ yí tiào
吓 我 一 跳 。

对牛弹琴

Play the lute to a cow.
Dway neo tahn cheen.

Meaning: Earnest expressions to the wrong audience.

To View

Gwahn

XIV. Places To Go-Things To See

■ Beijing *Bay jing*

▼ Sightseeing

Beijing Exhibition Center
Bay jing Jahn lahn Johng sheen
Běi jīng zhǎn lǎn zhōng xīn
北京 展 览 中 心

Beijing University
Bay jing Dah shweh
Běi jīng dà xué
北京 大 学

Beijing Zoo
Bay jing Dohng woo ywahn
Běi jīng dòng wù yuán
北京 动 物 园

China Art Gallery
Johng gwuh May shoo gwahn
Zhōng guó měi shù guǎn
中 国美术馆

Drum Tower & Bell Tower
Johng goo Loh
Zhōng gǔ lóu
钟 鼓 楼

Forbidden City
Goo gohng or **Zih jeen chung**
Gù gōng Zǐ jìn chéng
故 宫 ; 紫 禁 城

Fragrant Hills Park
Shee-ahng shahn Gohng ywahn
Xiāng shān gōng yuán
香 山 公 园

Great Bell Temple	***Dah johng Sih*** Dà zhōng sì 大 钟 寺
Lama Temple	***Yohng huh Gohng*** Yōng hé gōng 雍 和 宫
National Museum of Chinese History	***Johng gwuh Lee shir*** ***Boo woo gwahn*** Zhōng guó lì shǐ 中 国 历 史 bó wù guǎn 博 物 馆
Natural History Museum	***Zih rahn Boo woo gwahn*** Zì rán bó wù guǎn 自 然 博 物 馆
North Sea Park	***Bay hye Gohng ywahn*** Běi hǎi gōng yuán 北 海 公 园
Old Summer Palace	***Ywahn ming Ywahn*** Yuán míng yuán 圆 明 园
San Li Tun (Bar Area)	***Sahn lee twun*** ***Jeo bah Jee-eh*** Sān lǐ tún jiǔ bā jiē 三 里 屯 酒 吧 街
Shidu Village	***Shir Doo*** Shí dù 十 渡

Shishahai Park	***Shir chah hye*** ***Gohng ywahn*** Shí chà hǎi gōng yuán 什刹海公园
Summer Palace	***Ee huh ywahn Ee jir*** Yí hé yuán yí zhǐ 颐和园 遗址
Temple of Heaven Park	***Tee-en tahn Gohng ywahn*** Tiān tán gōng yuán 天坛公园
The Great Wall (at Ba Da Ling)	***Bah dah ling*** ***Chahng chung*** Bā dá lǐng cháng chéng 八达岭长城
The Great Wall (at Mu Tian Yu)	***Moo tee-en yiew*** ***Chahng chung*** Mù tián yù cháng chéng 慕田峪长城
The Thirteen Tombs	***Shir sahn Ling*** Shí sān líng 十三陵
Tian An Men Square	***Tee-en ahn men*** ***Gwahng chahng*** Tiān ān mén guǎng chǎng 天安门广场
Zheng Yi Ci Opera Theatre	***Jung yee tsih*** ***Dah shee loh*** Zhèng yǐ cí dà xì lóu 正乙祠大戏楼
Qing Hua University	***Ching hwah Dah shweh*** Qīng huá dà xué 清华大学

▼ Shopping

Silk Street	***Dah shir lah*** Dà shi la 大 栅 栏
Hong Qiao Market	***Hohng chee-aow Shir chahng*** Hóng qiáo shì chǎng 红 桥 市 场
Antique Street	***Leo lee Chahng*** Liú li chǎng 琉 璃 厂
Dirt Market	***Pahn jee-ah ywahn Shir chahng*** Pān jiā yuán shì chǎng 潘 家 园 市 场
Wang Fu Jing Shopping Street	***Wahng foo jing Dah jee-eh*** Wáng fǔ jīng dà jiē 王 府 井 大 街
Silk Market	***Sheo shway Shir chahng*** Xiù shuǐ shì chǎng 秀 水 市 场

▼ Embassies

American Embassy	***May gwuh Dah shir gwahn*** Měi guó dà shǐ guǎn 美 国 大 使 馆

Australian Embassy

Aow dah lee yah
Dah shir gwahn
Ao dà lì yà dà shǐ guǎn
澳 大 利 亚 大 使 馆

Canadian Embassy

Jee-ah nah dah
Dah shir gwahn
Jiā ná dà dà shǐ guǎn
加 拿 大 大 使 馆

Chinese Embassy

Johng gwuh
Dah shir gwahn
Zhōng guó dà shǐ guǎn
中 国 大 使 馆

French Embassy

Fah gwuh Dah shir gwahn
Fǎ guó dà shǐ guǎn
法 国 大 使 馆

German Embassy

Duh gwuh Dah shir gwahn
Dé guó dà shǐ guǎn
德 国 大 使 馆

Japanese Embassy

Rr ben Dah shir gwahn
Rì běn dà shǐ guǎn
日 本 大 使 馆

New Zealand Embassy

Sheen shee lahn
Dah shir gwahn
Xīn xī lán dà shǐ guǎn
新 西 兰 大 使 馆

Russian Embassy

Uh lwuh sih
Dah shir gwahn
E luó sī dà shǐ guǎn
俄 罗 斯 大 使 馆

Thai Embassy

Tye gwuh Dah shir gwahn
Tài guó dà shǐ guǎn
泰 国 大 使 馆

Vietnamese Embassy	***Yweh nahn***
	Dah shir gwahn
	Yuè nán dà shǐ guǎn
	越 南 大 使 馆
South Korean Embassy	***Hahn gwuh***
	Dah shir gwahn
	Hán guó dà shǐ guǎn
	韩 国 大 使 馆

▼ Other

Airport	***Fay jee chahng***
	fēi jī chǎng
	飞 机 场
Main Train Station	***Hwuh chuh jahn***
	huǒ chē zhàn
	火 车 站
West Train Station	***Bay jing Shee jahn***
	Běi jīng xī zhàn
	北 京 西 站

■ Guangzhou   *Gwahng joh*

Although Cantonese is predominantly spoken in Guangzhou, most locals also speak Mandarin.

▼ Sightseeing

Bright Filial Piety Temple	***Gwahng shee-aow Sih***
	Guāng xiào sì
	光 孝 寺

Cultural Park	**Wen hwah Gohng ywahn** Wén huà gōng yuán 文 化 公 园
Five Genies Temple	**Woo shee-en Gwahn** Wǔ xiān guàn 五 仙 观
Guangzhou Zoo	**Gwahng joh** **Dohng woo ywahn** Guǎng zhōu dòng wù yuán 广 州 动 物 园
Liuhua Lake Park	**Leo hwah hoo** **Gohng ywahn** Liú huā hú gōng yuán 流 花 湖 公 园
Our Lady of Lourdes Chapel	**Tee-en joo jee-aow loo** **Shung moo Tahng** Tiān zhǔ jiào lù shèng mǔ táng 天 主 教 露 圣 母 堂
Remember the Prophet Mosque	**Hwye shung sih** **Gwahng tah** Huái shèng sì guāng tǎ 怀 圣 寺 光 塔
Sacred Heart Church	**Shir shir Jee-aow tahng** Shí shì jiào táng 石 室 教 堂
Sand Surface Island	**Shah mee-en Daow** Shā miàn dǎo 沙 面 岛

Southern Yue Tomb Museum	*Nahn yweh wahng Hahn moo*
	Nán yuè wáng hàn mù
	南 越 王 汉 墓

Temple of the
Six Banyan Trees

Leo rohng Sih Hwah tah
Liù róng sì huā tǎ
六 榕 寺 花 塔

Yuexiu Park

*Yweh sheo
Gohng ywahn*
Yuè xiù gōng yuán
越 秀 公 园

▼ Shopping

Beijing Road
(Shopping Area)

Bay jing Loo
Běi jīng lù
北 京 路

Bright Peace Market

Ching ping Shir chahng
Qīng píng shì chǎng
清 平 市 场

Shang Jiu Road
(Shopping Area)

Shahng jeo Loo
Shàng jiǔ lù
上 九 路

Xia Jiu Road
(Shopping Area)

Shee-ah jeo Loo
Xià jiǔ lù
下 九 路

Zhong Shan Road
(Shopping Area)

Johng shahn Loo
Zhōng shān lù
中 山 路

▼ Consulates

American Consulate

May gwuh
Ling shir gwahn
Měi guó lǐng shì guǎn
美 国 领 事 馆

Australian Consulate

Aow dah lee yah
Ling shir gwahn
Ao dà lì yà lǐng shì guǎn
澳 大 利 亚 领 事 馆

Canadian Consulate

Jee-ah nah dah
Ling shir gwahn
Jiā ná dà lǐng shì guǎn
加 拿 大 领 事 馆

German Consulate

Duh gwuh
Ling shir gwahn
Dé guó lǐng shì guǎn
德 国 领 事 馆

Japanese Consulate

Rr ben Ling shir gwahn
Rì běn lǐng shì guǎn
日 本 领 事 馆

Polish Consulate

Bwuh lahn
Ling shir gwahn
Bō lán lǐng shì guǎn
波 兰 领 事 馆

Thai Consulate

Tye gwuh Ling shir gwahn
Tài guó lǐng shì guǎn
泰 国 领 事 馆

Vietnamese Consulate

Yweh nahn
Ling shir gwahn
Yuè nán lǐng shì guǎn
越 南 领 事 馆

▼ Others

Airport

Fay jee chahng
fēi jī chǎng
飞 机 场

Main Train Station

Gwahng joh
Hwuh chuh jahn
Guǎng zhōu huǒ chē zhàn
广　州　火 车 站

■ Nanjing

Nahn jing

Sightseeing

Bell Tower

Johng Loh
Zhōng lóu
钟　楼

Botanical Gardens

Jir woo Ywahn
Zhí wù yuán
植 物 园

Drum Tower

Goo Loh
Gǔ　lóu
鼓 楼

Heaven Dynasty Palace

Chaow tee-en Gohng
Cháo tiān gōng
朝 天 宫

Man and Son Temple

Foo zih Mee-aow
Fū zǐ miào
夫 子 庙

Memorial of the Nanjing Massacre	***Dah too shah Jee nee-en gwahn*** Dà tú shā jì niàn guǎn 大屠杀纪念馆
Ming City Wall	***Ming Chahng chung Ee jir*** Míng cháng chéng yí zhǐ 明长城遗址
Ming Palace Ruins	***Ming Goo gohng*** Míng gù gōng 明故宫
Morning of Birds Temple	***Chee shee-ah Shahn*** Qī xiá shān 栖霞山
Nanjing Museum	***Nahn jing Bwuh woo gwahn*** Nán jīng bó wù guǎn 南京博物馆
Nanjing University	***Nahn jing Dah shweh*** Nán jīng dà xué 南京大学
Scenic Spot of Ming Dynasty Tomb	***Ming Shee-aow ling Fung jing chiew*** Míng xiào líng fēng jǐng qū 明孝陵风景区
Spirit Valley Temple	***Ling goo Sih*** Líng gǔ sì 灵谷寺
Sun Yetsen Mausoleum	***Johng shahn Ling*** Zhōng shān líng 中山陵

Taiping Heavenly Kingdom
History Museum

Tye ping Tee-en gwuh
Lee shir Boo woo gwahn

Tài píng tiān guó
太 平 天 国
lì shǐ bó wù guǎn
历 史 博 物 馆

Yangzi River Bridge

Nahn jing
Chahng jee-ahng
Dah chee-aow

Nán jīng cháng jiāng dà qiáo
南 京 长 江 大 桥

▼ **Shopping**

Late Night Market

Hoo nahn Loo Yeh shir

Hú nán lù yè shì
湖 南 路 夜 市

Shopping Street

Johng shahn Loo

Zhōng shān lù
中 山 路

■ **Qingdao**　　*Ching daow*

▼ **Sightseeing**

Bathing Beach No 1, 2, 3,
4, 5, 6 (Respectively)

Dee ee (ar, sahn, sih,
woo,leo) Hye shway
Yiew chahng

Dì
第 1（2，3，4，5，6）
hǎi shuǐ yù chǎng
海 水 浴 场

143

Northern Nine-Waterfalls   ***Bay jeo shway***
Běi jiǔ shuǐ
北 九 水

Catholic Church   ***Tee-en joo Jee-aow tahng***
Tiān zhǔ jiào táng
天 主 教 堂

Lao Shan Retreat   ***Laow Shahn***
Láo   shān
崂 山

Lu Xun Park   ***Loo shwin Gohng ywahn***
Lǔ   xùn gōng yuán
鲁 迅 公 园

Ocean Park   ***Hye yahng Gohng ywahn***
Hǎi yáng gōng yuán
海 洋 公 园

Old Stone Man
Bathing Beach   ***Shir laow ren Yiew chahng***
Shí lǎo rén yù chǎng
石 老 人 浴 场

Protestant Church   ***Jee doo Jee-aow tahng***
Jī   dū   jiào táng
基 督 教 堂

Taipingshan Park   ***Tye ping shahn***
Gohng ywahn
tài píng shān gōng yuán
太 平 山 公 园

The Aquatic Museum   ***Hye chahn***
Bwuh woo gwahn
Hǎi chǎn bó wù guǎn
海 产 博 物 馆

The German Governor's
Residence

Hwah shir Loh
Huā shí lóu
花 石 楼

Xinhaoshan Park

**Sheen haow shahn
Gohng ywahn**
Xìn hào shān gōng yuán
信 号 山 公 园

Xinhaoshan
Guest House

**Sheen haow shahn
Ying been gwahn**
Xìn hào shān yíng bīn guǎn
信 号 山 迎 宾 馆

Zhongshan Park

**Johng shahn
Gohng ywahn**
Zhōng shān gōng yuán
中 山 公 园

▼ Shopping

Jimo Lu Market

**Jee mwoh Loo
Shir chahng**
Jí mò lù shì chǎng
即 墨 路 市 场

Taidong Walking Street

**Tye dohng
Boo shing Jee-eh**
Tái dōng bù xíng jiē
台 东 步 行 街

Zhong Shan Road
Shopping Street

**Johng shahn Loo
Shahng yee-eh Jee-eh**
Zhōng shān lù shāng yè jiē
中 山 路 商 业 街

145

▼ **Other**

Tsingtao Brewery

Ching daow
Pee jeo chahng
Qīng dǎo pí jiǔ chǎng
青 岛 啤 酒 厂

Yan'an Er'lu Night Market

Yahn ahn Ar loo
Yee-eh shir
Yán ān èr lù yè shì
延 安 二 路 夜 市

■ **Shanghai**   *Shahng hye*

▼ **Sightseeing**

Botanical Gardens

Jir woo Ywahn
Zhí wù yuán
植 物 园

Exhibition Center

Jahn lahn Johng sheen
Zhǎn lǎn zhōng xīn
展 览 中 心

Hengshan Rd.

Hung shahn Loo
Héng shān lù
衡 山 路

History Museum

Lee shir Bwuh woo gwahn
Lì shǐ bó wù guǎn
历 史 博 物 馆

Huangpu Park

Hwahng poo
Gohng ywahn
Huáng pǔ gōng yuán
黄 浦 公 园

Jade Buddha Temple *Yiew fwuh Sih*
Yù fó sì
玉 佛 寺

Longhua Pagoda *Lohng hwah Tah*
Lóng huá tǎ
龙 华 塔

Old Street *Laow Jee-eh*
Lǎo jiē
老 街

Oriental Pearl Tower *Dohng fahng ming joo*
Dōng fāng míng zhū
东 方 明 珠

Renmin Park *Ren meen Gohng ywahn*
Rén mín gōng yuán
人 民 公 园

Temple of the Town Gods *Chung hwahng Mee-aow*
Chéng huáng miào
城 隍 庙

The Bund *Wye tahn*
Wài tān
外 滩

The French Concessions *Fah gwuh Zoo jee-eh*
Fǎ guó zū jiè
法 国 租 界

Yu Gardens Bazaar *Yiew Ywahn*
Yù yuán
豫 园

Zoo *Dohng woo Ywahn*
Dòng wù yuán
动 物 园

▼ Shopping

Dongtai Lu Antique Market **Dohng tye Loo Goo wahn Shir chahng**
Dōng tái lù gǔ wán shì chǎng
东 台 路 古 玩 市 场

Fangbang Rd.
Antique Market
Fahng bahng Loo Goo wahn Shir chahng
Fāng bāng lù gǔ wán shì chǎng
方 浜 路 古 玩 市 场

Foreign Languages
Bookstore
Wye wen Shoo dee-en
Wài wén shū diàn
外 文 书 店

Huaihai Rd. **Hwye hye Loo**
Huái hǎi lù
淮 海 路

Isetan Department Store **Ee shir dahn**
Yī shì dān
伊 势 丹

Nanjing Rd. **Nahn jing Loo**
Nán jīng lù
南 京 路

Yandang Lu **Yahn dahng Loo**
Yàn dàng lù
雁 荡 路

▼ Entertainment

Cathay Theatre **Gwuh tye Dee-en ying ywahn**
Guó tài diàn yǐng yuàn
国 泰 电 影 院

148

Great World   **_Dah shir jee-eh_**
Dà shì jiè
大 世 界

Lyceum Theatre   **_Lahn sheen_**
Dah shee ywahn
Lán xīn dà xì yuàn
兰 心 大 戏 院

Shanghai Grand Theatre   **_Shahng hye_**
Dah jiew ywahn
Shàng hǎi dà jù yuàn
上 海 大 剧 院

▼ Transportation

Hongqiao Airport   **_Hohng chee-aow_**
Jee chahng
Hóng qiáo jī chǎng
虹 桥 机 场

Pudong Airport   **_Poo dohng Jee chahng_**
Pǔ dōng jī chǎng
浦 东 机 场

Sichuan Zhong Rd.
Train Ticket Booking
Service   **_Sih chwahn Johng loo_**
Hwuh chuh Shoh
pee-aow choo
Sì chuān zhōng lù
四 川 中 路
huǒ chē shòu piào chù
火 车 售 票 处

Sightseeing Bus Center   **_Liew yoh Jee sahn_**
Johng sheen
Lǚ you jí sàn zhōng xīn
旅 游 集 散 中 心

South Train Station

Shahng hye Nahn Jahn
Shàng hǎi nán zhàn
上　海南站

West Train Station

Shahng hye Shee Jahn
Shàng hǎi xī　zhàn
上　海西站

Western District
Bus Station

Shee chiew
Chee chuh jahn
Xī　qū　qì chē zhàn
西区汽车站

▼ Consulates

American Consulate

May gwuh
Ling shir gwahn
Měi guó lǐng shì guǎn
美国 领 事 馆

Australian Consulate

Aow dah lee yah
Ling shir gwahn
Ao dà lì yà lǐng shì guǎn
澳 大 利 亚 领 事 馆

British Consulate

Ying gwuh
Ling shir gwahn
Yīng guó lǐng shì guǎn
英 国 领 事 馆

Canadian Consulate

Jee-ah nah dah
Ling shir gwahn
Jiā ná dà lǐng shì guǎn
加 拿 大 领 事 馆

French Consulate	***Fah gwuh Ling shir gwahn*** Fǎ guó lǐng shì guǎn 法 国 领 事 馆
German Consulate	***Duh gwuh*** ***Ling shir gwahn*** Dé guó lǐng shì guǎn 德 国 领 事 馆
Japanese Consulate	***Rr ben Ling shir gwahn*** Rì běn lǐng shì guǎn 日 本 领 事 馆
New Zealand Consulate	***Sheen shee lahn*** ***Ling shir gwahn*** Xīn xī lán lǐng shì guǎn 新 西 兰 领 事 馆
Russian Consulate	***Uh lwuh sih*** ***Ling shir gwahn*** E luó sī lǐng shì guǎn 俄 罗 斯 领 事 馆
South Korean Consulate	***Hahn gwuh*** ***Ling shir gwahn*** Hán guó lǐng shì guǎn 韩 国 领 事 馆

■ Tianjin   *Tee-en jeen*

▼ Sightseeing

Confucius Temple	***Wen Mee-aow*** Wén miào 文 庙

Jixian Village	**Jee Shee-en** Jì xiàn 蓟 县
Natural History Museum	**Zih rahn Boo woo gwahn** Zì rán bó wù guǎn 自 然 博 物 馆
Pan Shan (Mountain)	**Pahn Shahn** Pán shān 盘 山
The Great Wall at Yellow Cliff Pass	**Hwahng yah gwahn** **Chahng chung** Huáng yá guān cháng chéng 黄 崖 关 长 城
The Qing Tombs	**Qing dohng Ling** Qīng dōng líng 清 东 陵
Tianjin Zoo	**Tee-en jing** **Dohng woo ywahn** Tiān jīn dòng wù yuán 天 津 动 物 园
Water Park	**Shway shahng** **Gohng ywahn** Shuǐ shàng gōng yuán 水 上 公 园
Wu Da Dao (European Concession)	**Woo Dah Daow** Wǔ dà dào 五 大 道
Zhou Enlai Memorial Hall	**Joh En lye** **Jee nee-en gwahn** Zhōu ēn lái jì niàn guǎn 周 恩 来 纪 念 馆

▼ Shopping

Ancient Culture Street

Goo wen hwah Jee-eh
Gǔ wén huà jiē
古 文 化 街

Bali Tai Culture Market

Bah lee tye
Wen hwah Shir chahng
Bā lǐ tái wén huà shì chǎng
八 里 台 文 化 市 场

Binjiang Street
(Shopping Street)

Been jee-ahng Daow
Bīn jiāng dào
滨 江 道

Friendship Store

Yoh ee Shahng dee-en
Yǒu yì shāng diàn
友 谊 商 店

Shenyang Street
(Antique Market)

Shen yahng Daow
Shěn yáng dào
沈 阳 道

▼ Other

Main Train Station

Tee-en jeen Dohng Jahn
Tiān jīn dōng zhàn
天 津 东 站

West Train Station

Tee-en jeen Shee Jahn
Tiān jīn xī zhàn
天 津 西 站

153

Foreign Language Institute **Wye gwuh yiew**
Shweh ywahn
Wài guó yǔ xué yuàn
外 国 语 学 院

Nankai University **Nahn kye Dah shweh**
Nán kāi dà xué
南 开 大 学

Tianjin University **Tee-en jeen Dah shweh**
Tiān jīn dà xué
天 津 大 学

■ Xi'an **Shee ahn**

▼ Sightseeing

Army of Terracotta **Bing mah yohng**
Warriors **Bwuh woo gwahn**
Bīng mǎ yǒng bó wù guǎn
兵 马 俑 博 物 馆

Banpo Neolithic Village **Bahn pwuh Ee jir**
Bàn pō yí zhǐ
半 坡 遗 址

Bell Tower **Johng Loh**
Zhōng lóu
钟 楼

Big Goose Pagoda **Dah yahn Tah**
Dà yàn tǎ
大 雁 塔

City God's Temple **Chung hwahng Mee-aow**
Chéng huáng miào
城 隍 庙

City Walls   **Chung chee-ahng**
Chéng qiáng
城　墙

Drum Tower   **Goo Loh**
Gǔ lóu
鼓 楼

Forest of Steles Museum   **Bay leen Boo woo gwahn**
Bēi lín bó wù guǎn
碑 林 博 物 馆

Great Mosque   **Dah Ching jen sih**
Dà qīng zhēn sì
大 清 真 寺

Huajuexiang Market   **Hwah jweh Shee-ahng**
Huà jué xiàng
化 觉 巷

Huaqing Pool   **Hwah ching Chir**
Huá qīng chí
华 清 池

Hua Shan Mountain   **Hwah Shahn**
Huá shān
华 山

Little Goose Pagoda   **Shee-aow yahn Tah**
Xiǎo yàn tǎ
小 雁 塔

Shaan Xi History Museum   **Shahn shee Lee shir Boo woo gwahn**
Shǎn xī lì shǐ bó wù guǎn
陕 西 历 史 博 物 馆

Temple of the
Eight Immortals

Bah shee-en Ahn
Bā xiān ān
八 仙 庵

Tomb of Qin ShiHuang

Cheen shir hwahng Ling
Qín shǐ huáng líng
秦 始 皇 陵

■ Other Tourist Areas / Cities in China

Chengde (Bishu
Shanzhuang Summer
Palace)

**Chung duh Bee shoo
Shahn jwahng**
Chéng dé bì shǔ shān zhuāng
承 德 避 暑 山 庄

Grand Buddha
(Si Chuan Province)

**Luh shahn Dah fwuh
(Sih chwahn Shung)**
Lè shān dà fó
乐 山 大 佛
Sì chuān shěng
(四 川 省)

Dali Village
(Yun Nan Province)

**Dah lee
(Ywin nahn Shung)**
Dà lǐ   Yún nán shěng
大 理 (云 南 省)

Dunhuang
(Gansu Province)

**Dwun hwahng
(Gahn soo Shung)**
Dūn huáng   Gān sù shěng
敦 煌 (甘 肃 省)

Inner Mongolia

Nay mung goo
Nèi měng gǔ
内 蒙 古

Jiuzhai Gou
(Si Chuan Province)

Jeo jye goh
(Sih chwahn Shung)
Jiǔ zhài gōu
九 寨 沟
Sì chuān shěng
（四 川 省 ）

Lhasa
(Tibet)

La sah
(Shee zahng shoh foo)
Lā sà　　Xī zàng shǒu fǔ
拉 萨（西 藏 首 府 ）

Lijiang Village
(Yun Nan Province)

Lee jee-ahng
(Ywin nahn Shung)
Lì jiāng　　Yún nán shěng
丽 江 （ 云 南 省 ）

Tibet

Shee zahng
Xī zàng
西 藏

Wulumuqi
(capital of Xinjiang)

Woo loo moo chee
(Sheen jee-ahng shoh foo)
Wū lǔ mù qí
乌 鲁 木 齐
Xīn jiāng shǒu fǔ
（ 新 疆 首 府 ）

Xinjiang

Sheen jee-ahng
Xīn jiāng
新 疆

Xishuang ban'na Region

Shee shwahng bahn nah
Xī shuāng bǎn nà
西 双 版 纳

Yangshuo Village
(Guangxi Province)

Yahng shwuh
(Gwahng shee Shung)

Yáng shuò   Guǎng xī   sheng
阳   朔（广   西 省 ）

Yungang Shiku Buddhist
Caves (Shanxi Province)

Ywin gahng Shir koo
(Shahn shee Shung)

Yún gāng shí kū
云 冈   石 窟

Shān xī   shěng
（山 西 省 ）

读万卷书

行万里路

Read ten thousand books,
travel ten thousand miles.
Doo wahn jwahn shoo, shing wahn lee loo.

Vocabulary

Vocabulary

abacus	*swahn pahn*	suàn pán 算 盘
abortion	*leo chahn*	liú chǎn 流 产
about	*dah yweh*	dà yuē 大 约
about (things)	*gwahn yiew*	guān yú 关 于
abroad	*gwuh wye*	guó wài 国 外
accept	*jee-eh shoh*	jiē shòu 接 受
accident	*ee wye*	yì wài 意 外
accommodation	*joo choo*	zhù chù 住 处
accurate	*jwun chweh*	zhǔn què 准 确
achievement	*chung jeo*	chéng jiù 成 就
acupuncture	*jen jeo*	zhēn jiǔ 针 灸
additional	*uh wye duh*	é wài de 额 外 的
address book	*tohng shwin boo*	tōng xùn bù 通 讯 簿
address	*dee jir*	dì zhǐ 地 址
adult	*chung ren*	chéng rén 成 人

| aerobics | *yoh yahng - jee-en shen* | yǒu yǎng jiàn shēn 有 氧 健 身 |
| afraid | | |

aerobics	*yoh yahng - jee-en shen*	yǒu yǎng jiàn shēn 有 氧 健 身
Afghanistan	*Ah foo hahn*	A fù hàn 阿 富 汗
afraid	*hye pah*	hài pà 害 怕
African	*Fay joh*	Fēi zhōu 非 洲
after	*zye___jir hoh*	zài ___ zhī hòu 在 ___ 之 后
afternoon	*shee-ah woo*	xià wǔ 下 午
again	*yoh*	yòu 又
against	*fahn dway*	fǎn duì 反 对
agency	*dye lee choo*	dài lǐ chù 代 理 处
agent	*dye lee shahng*	dài lǐ shāng 代 理 商
agree	*tohng ee*	tóng yì 同 意
air conditioning	*kohng tee-aow*	kōng tiáo 空 调
air	*kohng chee*	kōng qì 空 气
airmail	*hahng kohng - yoh jee-en*	háng kōng yóu jiàn 航 空 邮 件
airplane	*fay jee*	fēi jī 飞 机

airport	*fay jee chahng*	fēi jī chǎng 飞 机 场
alarm (noun)	*jing baow*	jǐng bào 警 报
alarm clock	*naow johng*	nào zhōng 闹 钟
alcohol	*jeo*	jiǔ 酒
all	*doh*	dōu 都
allergic	*gwuh meen*	guò mǐn 过 敏
allow	*ywun shiew*	yǔn xǔ 允 许
almost	*chah boo dwuh*	chà bu duō 差 不 多
always	*zohng shir*	zǒng shì 总 是
ambulance	*jeo hoo chuh*	jiù hù chē 救 护 车
America	*May gwuh*	Měi guó 美 国
American (people)	*May gwuh ren*	Měi guó rén 美 国 人
Amsterdam	*Ah moo - sih tuh dahn*	A mǔ sī tè dān 阿 姆 斯 特 丹
ancient	*goo dye duh*	gǔ dài de 古 代 的
and	*huh*	hé 和
angry	*shung chee*	shēng qì 生 气

animal	*dohng woo*	dòng wù 动 物
another	*ling ee guh*	lìng yí gè 另 一 个
answer (noun)	*dah ahn*	dá àn 答 案
answer (verb)	*hway dah*	huí dá 回 答
antibiotics	*kahng shung soo*	kàng shēng sù 抗 生 素
antique store	*goo dohng - dee-en*	gǔ dǒng diàn 古 董 店
any	*ren huh*	rèn hé 任 何
apartment	*gohng yiew*	gōng yù 公 寓
apple	*ping gwuh*	píng guǒ 苹 果
appointment	*yweh hway*	yuē huì 约 会
appreciate	*gahn jee*	gǎn jī 感 激
approve	*pee jwun*	pī zhǔn 批 准
apricot	*shing*	xìng 杏
April	*Sih yweh*	sì yuè 四 月
Argentina	*Ah gen ting*	A gēn tíng 阿 根 廷
argue	*jung lwun*	zhēng lùn 争 论

arm	*guh bwuh*	gē bo 胳 膊
arrive	*daow dah*	dào dá 到 达
art gallery	*hwah lahng*	huà láng 画 廊
art museum	*may shoo bwuh woo gwahn*	měi shù bó wù guǎn 美 术 博 物 馆
art	*ee shoo*	yì shù 艺 术
artist	*ee shoo jee-ah*	yì shù jiā 艺 术 家
arts and crafts	*gohng ee peen*	gōng yì pǐn 工 艺 品
Asia	*Yah joh*	Yà zhōu 亚 洲
ask	*wen*	wèn 问
asparagus	*loo swen*	lú sǔn 芦 笋
aspirin	*ah sih pee leen*	ā sī pǐ lín 阿 斯 匹 林
ass	*pee goo*	pì gu 屁 股
asshole (bastard)	*hwun dahn*	hún dàn 混 蛋
asthma	*shee-aow chwahn*	xiào chuǎn 哮 喘

ATM machine	*zih dohng -*	zì dòng 自动
	chiew kwahn jee	qǔ kuǎn jī 取款机
attorney	*liew shir*	lǜ shī 律师
attractive	*yoh may lee duh*	yǒu mèi lì de 有魅力的
August	*Bah yweh*	bā yuè 八月
Australian (people)	*Aow dah lee - yah ren*	Ao dà lì yà rén 澳大利亚人
Austria	*Aow dee lee*	Ao dì lì 奥地利
automobile	*chee chuh*	qì chē 汽车
avenue	*dah jee-eh*	dà jiē 大街
awake	*shing juh*	xǐng zhe 醒着
baby food	*ying ar shir peen*	yīng ér shí pǐn 婴儿食品
baby	*ying ar*	yīng ér 婴儿
back (body)	*hoh bay*	hòu bèi 后背
back	*hoh mee-en duh*	hòu mian de 后面的
bad	*hwye*	huài 坏
bag	*baow*	bāo 包

baggage cart	*shing lee chuh*	xíng li chē 行 李 车
baggage check	*shing lee -* *twuh ywin dahn*	xíng li 行 李 tuō yùn dān 托 运 单
baggage claim department	*shing lee -* *twuh ywin choo*	xíng li 行 李 tuō yùn chù 托 运 处
baggage	*shing lee*	xíng li 行 李
bakery	*mee-en baow -* *dee-en*	miàn bāo diàn 面 包 店
ball game, match	*cheo sye*	qiú sài 球 赛
ball	*cheo*	qiú 球
ballpoint pen	*ywahn joo bee*	yuán zhū bǐ 圆 珠 笔
bamboo shoot	*joo swun*	zhú sǔn 竹 笋
banana	*shee-ahng -* *jee-aow*	xiāng jiāo 香 蕉
bandage	*bung dye*	bēng dài 绷 带
band-aid	*chwahng kuh -* *tee-eh*	chuàng kě tiē 创 可 贴
bank	*yeen hahng*	yín háng 银 行
banquet	*yahn hway*	yàn huì 宴 会

bar	*jeo bah*	jiǔ bā 酒 吧
barbecue	*shaow kaow*	shāo kǎo 烧 烤
barber shop	*lee fah dee-en*	lǐ fà diàn 理 发 店
barber	*lee fah shir*	lǐ fà shī 理 发 师
baseball	*bahng cheo*	bàng qiú 棒 球
basketball match	*lahn cheo -bee sye*	lán qiú bǐ sài 篮 球 比 赛
basketball	*lahn cheo*	lán qiú 篮 球
bath towel	*yiew jeen*	yù jīn 浴 巾
bathe	*shee zaow*	xǐ zǎo 洗 澡
bathing suit	*yoh yohng ee*	yóu yǒng yī 游 泳 衣
bathrobe	*yiew ee*	yù yī 浴 衣
bathroom	*shee shoh jee-en*	xǐ shǒu jiān 洗 手 间
bathtub	*yiew gahng*	yù gāng 浴 缸
battery	*dee-en chir*	diàn chí 电 池
beach	*hye tahn*	hǎi tān 海 滩
bean curd	*doh foo*	dòu fǔ 豆 腐

English	Pronunciation	Pinyin / Chinese
bean sprout	*doh yah*	dòu yá 豆芽
beat, win	*ying*	yíng 赢
beautiful	*pee-aow - lee-ahng*	piào liang 漂 亮
beauty (girl)	*may ren*	měi rén 美 人
beauty salon	*may rohng - ywahn*	měi róng yuàn 美 容 院
because	*yeen way*	yīn wéi 因 为
bedroom	*wuh shir*	wò shì 卧 室
bed sheet	*chwahng dahn*	chuáng dān 床 单
bed	*chwahng*	chuáng 床
bedbugs	*choh chohng*	chòu chóng 臭 虫
beef	*neo roh*	niú ròu 牛 肉
beer	*pee jeo*	pí jiǔ 啤 酒
beggar	*chee gye*	qǐ gài 乞 丐
behind	*zye__ hoh - mee-en*	zài ___ hòu miàn 在 ___后 面
Beijing	*Bay jing*	Běi jīng 北 京
Belgium	*Bee lee shir*	Bǐ lì shí 比 利 时

belt	*yaow dye*	yāo dài 腰 带
beside, next to	*zye___ pahng - bee-en*	zài　páng biān 在__旁 边
best	*zway haow duh*	zuì hǎo de 最 好 的
better	*gung haow duh*	gèng hǎo de 更 好 的
between	*zye___jir jee-en*	zài　zhī jiān 在__之 间
big	*dah*	dà 大
bigger	*gung dah duh*	gèng dà　de 更 大 的
bike	*zih shing chuh*	zì xíng chē 自 行 车
bill	*jahng dahn*	zhàng dān 帐 单
birth control	*jee hwah - shung yiew*	jì huà shēng yù 计 划 生 育
birthday	*shung rr*	shēng rì 生 日
bitter	*koo duh*	kǔ de 苦 的
black	*hay suh duh*	hēi sè de 黑 色 的
blanket	*tahn zih*	tǎn zi 毯 子
bleed	*leo shweh*	liú xuè 流 血
blood pressure	*shweh yah*	xuè yā 血 压

blood type	*shweh shing*	xuè xíng 血 型
blood	*shweh*	xuè 血
blue	*lahn suh duh*	lán sè de 蓝 色 的
boat	*chwahn*	chuán 船
body temperature	*tee wen*	tǐ wēn 体 温
body	*shen tee*	shēn tǐ 身 体
boil (verb)	*joo*	zhǔ 煮
boiled water	*kye shway*	kāi shuǐ 开 水
Bombay	*Mung mye*	Mèng mǎi 孟 买
bon voyage	*ee loo ping ahn*	yí lù píng ān 一 路 平 安
book	*shoo*	shū 书
bookstore	*shoo dee-en*	shū diàn 书 店
boot	*shweh zih*	xuē zi 靴 子
borrow	*jee-eh*	jiè 借
boss	*laow bahn*	lǎo bǎn 老 板
bottle opener	*chee ping chee*	qǐ píng qì 启 瓶 器

bottle	*ping zih*	píng zi 瓶 子	
bowl	*wahn*	wǎn 碗	
box	*huh zih*	hé zi 盒 子	
boy	*nahn hye*	nán hái 男 孩	
boyfriend	*nahn pung yoh*	nán péng you 男 朋 友	
bra	*roo jaow*	rǔ zhào 乳 罩	
brag	*chway neo*	chuī niú 吹 牛	
brand, trademark	*shahng bee-aow*	shāng biāo 商 标	
Brazil	*Bah shee*	Bā xī 巴 西	
bread	*mee-en baow*	miàn bāo 面 包	
breakfast	*zaow tsahn*	zǎo cān 早 餐	
breast ("milk house")	*roo fahng*	rǔ fáng 乳 房	
breathe	*hoo shee*	hū xī 呼 吸	
bride	*sheen nee-ahng*	xīn niáng 新 娘	
bridegroom	*sheen lahng*	xīn láng 新 郎	
bring	*nah lye*	ná lái 拿 来	

British	*Ying gwuh*	Yīng guó 英 国
broken	*hwye luh*	huài le 坏 了
broccoli	*shee lahn hwah*	xī lán huā 西 兰 花
broiled	*kaow*	kǎo 烤
brother	*shee-ohng dee*	xiōng dì 兄 弟
brown	*zohng suh duh*	zōng sè de 棕 色 的
Buddhism	*Fwuh jee-aow*	Fó jiào 佛 教
Buddhist	*Fwuh jee-aow - too*	Fó jiào tú 佛 教 徒
budget	*yiew swahn*	yù suàn 预 算
buffet	*zih joo tsahn*	zì zhù cān 自 助 餐
building	*loh*	lóu 楼
bullshit	*chuh dahn*	chě dàn 扯 淡
Burma	*Mee-en dee-en*	Miǎn diàn 缅 甸
burn (injury)	*shaow shahng*	shāo shāng 烧 伤
bus	*gohng gohng - chee chuh*	gōng gòng qì chē 公 共 汽 车
business	*shung ee*	shēng yì 生 意

business person	*shung ee ren*	shēng yì rén 生 意 人
busy	*mahng*	máng 忙
but	*dahn shir*	dàn shì 但 是
butter	*hwahng yoh*	huáng yóu 黄 油
buy	*mye*	mǎi 买
cabbage	*bye tsye*	bái cài 白 菜
cabin	*shee-aow woo*	xiǎo wū 小 屋
cable television	*yoh shee-en - dee-en shir*	yǒu xiàn diàn shì 有 线 电 视
café	*kah fay gwahn*	kā fēi guǎn 咖 啡 馆
Cairo	*Kye lwuh*	Kāi luó 开 罗
cake	*dahn gaow*	dàn gāo 蛋 糕
calculator	*jee swahn chee*	jì suàn qì 计 算 器
calendar	*rr lee*	rì lì 日 历
California	*Jee-ah joh*	Jiā zhōu 加 州
call ___(phone)	*gay ___ dah - dee-en hwah*	gěi dǎ diàn huà 给___打 电 话
calligraphy	*shoo fah*	shū fǎ 书 法

Cambodia	*Jee-en poo jye*	Jiǎn pǔ zhài 柬 埔 寨
camera	*jaow shee-ahng - jee*	zhào xiàng jī 照 相 机
can	*nung*	néng 能
can opener	*kye gwahn chee*	kāi guàn qì 开 罐 器
can, tin, jar	*gwahn zih*	guàn zi 罐 子
Canada	*Jee-ah nah dah*	Jiā ná dà 加 拿 大
Canberra	*Kahn pay lah*	Kǎn péi lā 堪 培 拉
cancel	*chiew shee-aow*	qǔ xiāo 取 消
cancer	*eye jung*	ái zhèng 癌 症
candle	*lah joo*	là zhú 蜡 烛
candy	*tahng gwuh*	táng guǒ 糖 果
capital (city)	*shoh doo*	shǒu dū 首 都
car	*chee chuh*	qì chē 汽 车
carpet	*dee tahn*	dì tǎn 地 毯
carrot	*hoo lwuh buh*	hú luó bo 胡 萝 卜
cash (noun)	*shee-en jeen*	xiàn jīn 现 金

cashier	*shoh kwahn - ywahn*	shōu kuǎn yuán 收 款 员
cassette tape	*loo yeen dye*	lù yīn dài 录 音 带
cat	*maow*	māo 猫
Catholic	*Tee-en joo - jee-aow too*	Tiān zhǔ jiào tú 天 主 教 徒
ceiling	*tee-en hwah - bahn*	tiān huā bǎn 天 花 板
celery	*cheen tsye*	qín cài 芹 菜
cent	*fen*	fēn 分
centigrade	*shuh shir doo*	shè shì dù 摄 氏 度
central heating	*jee johng - gohng ruh*	jí zhōng gōng rè 集 中 供 热
ceremony	*dee-en lee*	diǎn lǐ 典 礼
chair	*ee zih*	yǐ zi 椅 子
change (money)	*ling chee-en*	líng qián 零 钱
change (verb)	*hwahn*	huàn 换
cheap	*pee-en ee*	pián yi 便 宜
check (money)	*jir pee-aow*	zhī piào 支 票
check (verb)	*jee-en chah*	jiǎn chá 检 查

check-in	*dung jee*	dēng jì 登 记
chess	*shee-ahng chee*	xiàng qí 象 棋
chest cramp	*sheen jee-aow - tohng*	xīn jiǎo tòng 心 绞 痛
Chicago	*Jir jee-ah guh*	Zhī jiā gē 芝 加 哥
chicken	*jee*	jī 鸡
child	*hye zih*	hái zi 孩 子
chili	*hohng - lah jee-aow*	hóng là jiāo 红 辣 椒
China	*Johng gwuh*	Zhōng guó 中 国
Chinese language	*Johng wen*	Zhōng wén 中 文
Chinese(people)	*Johng gwuh ren*	Zhōng guó rén 中 国 人
chocolate	*chee-aow kuh - lee*	qiǎo kè lì 巧 克 力
chopsticks	*kwye zih*	kuài zǐ 筷 子
Christian	*Jee doo too*	Jī dū tú 基 督 徒
Christmas	*Shung dahn - Jee-eh*	shèng dàn jié 圣 诞 节
church	*jee-aow tahng*	jiào táng 教 堂
cigarette	*shee-ahng - yee-en*	xiāng yān 香 烟

city	*chung shir*	chéng shì 城 市
classmate	*tohng shweh*	tóng xué 同 学
clay figure	*nee ren*	ní rén 泥 人
clean	*gahn jing*	gàn jìng 干 净
climate	*chee hoh*	qì hòu 气 候
cloakroom (station)	*shing lee -*	xíng li 行 李
	jee tswen choo	jì cún chù 寄 存 处
clock	*johng*	zhōng 钟
closing time	*gwahn men - shir jee-en*	guān mén shí jiān 关 门 时 间
cloth	*boo*	bù 布
clothing	*ee foo*	yī fu 衣 服
cloud	*ywen*	yún 云
club	*jiew luh boo*	jù lè bù 俱 乐 部
coach bus	*chahng too - kuh chuh*	cháng tú kè chē 长 途 客 车
coal	*may*	méi 煤
coat hanger	*ee foo jee-ah*	yī fu jià 衣 服 架
coat	*dah ee*	dà yī 大 衣

cockroach	*jahng lahng*	zhāng láng 蟑 螂
cocktail	*jee way jeo*	jī wěi jiǔ 鸡 尾 酒
coffee shop	*kah fay gwahn*	kā fēi guǎn 咖 啡 馆
coffee	*kah fay*	kā fēi 咖 啡
coins	*ying bee*	yìng bì 硬 币
cold (illness)	*gahn maow*	gǎn mào 感 冒
cold	*lung*	lěng 冷
collect call	*dway fahng foo kwahn dee-en hwah*	duì fāng fù kuǎn 对 方 付 款 diàn huà 电 话
college, university	*dah shweh*	dà xué 大 学
Colombia	*Guh lwen - bee yah*	Gē lún bǐ yà 哥 伦 比 亚
color	*yahn suh*	yán sè 颜 色
comb	*shoo zih*	shū zi 梳 子
come	*lye*	lái 来
comedy	*shee jiew*	xǐ jù 喜 剧
comfortable	*shoo foo*	shū fu 舒 服

common	*poo tohng duh*	pǔ tōng de 普通的
communication	*goh tohng*	gōu tōng 沟通
Communist Party	*Gohng chahn - Dahng*	Gòng chǎn dǎng 共产党
company, firm	*gohng sih*	gōng sī 公司
complex	*foo zah duh*	fù zá de 复杂的
computer ("electronic brain")	*dee-en naow*	diàn nǎo 电脑
laptop computer	*bee jee ben - dee-en naow*	bǐ jì běn 笔记本 diàn nǎo 电脑
desktop computer	*tye shir - dee-en naow*	tái shì diàn nǎo 台式电脑
comrade	*tohng jir*	tóng zhì 同志
concert	*yeen yweh - hway*	yīn yuè huì 音乐会
condom	*bee ywen taow*	bì yùn tào 避孕套
conference room	*hway ee shir*	huì yì shì 会议室
confident	*zih sheen*	zì xìn 自信
Confucius	*Kohng zih*	Kǒng zǐ 孔子

congratulations	*gohng shee*	gōng xǐ 恭 喜
constipation	*bee-en mee*	biàn mì 便 秘
consulate	*ling shir gwahn*	lǐng shì guǎn 领 事 馆
contact lenses	*yeen shing - yahn jing*	yǐn xíng yǎn jìng 隐形 眼镜
contact	*lee-en shee*	lián xì 联 系
contagious	*hway chwahn - rahn duh*	huì chuán rǎn de 会 传 染 的
contraceptive	*bee ywen yaow*	bì yùn yào 避 孕 药
contract	*huh tohng*	hé tong 合 同
conversation	*tahn hwah*	tán huà 谈 话
cook (verb)	*zwuh fahn*	zuò fàn 做 饭
corn	*yiew mee*	yù mǐ 玉 米
correct (adj.)	*jung chweh duh*	zhèng què de 正 确 的
cost (noun)	*chung ben*	chéng běn 成 本
cost (verb)	*hwah fay*	huā fèi 花 费
cough	*kuh soh*	ké sou 咳 嗽
count	*shoo*	shǔ 数

English	Pronunciation	Chinese
country (nation)	*gwuh jee-ah*	guó jiā 国 家
countryside	*nohng tswun*	nóng cūn 农 村
couple (two)	*lee-ahng guh*	liǎng gè 两 个
courtyard	*ywahn zih*	yuàn zǐ 院 子
cow	*moo neo*	mǔ niú 母 牛
crab	*pahng shee-eh*	páng xiè 螃 蟹
cramps	*choh jeen*	chōu jīn 抽 筋
crazy	*fung luh*	fēng le 疯 了
cream	*nye yoh*	nǎi yóu 奶 油
create	*chwahng zaow*	chuàng zào 创 造
credit card	*sheen yohng kah*	xìn yòng kǎ 信 用 卡
cricket (sport)	*bahn cheo*	bǎn qiú 板 球
crowded	*yohng jee*	yōng jǐ 拥 挤
Cuba	*Goo bah*	Gǔ bā 古 巴
cucumber	*hwahng gwah*	huáng guā 黄 瓜
cuddle	*yohng baow*	yōng bào 拥 抱

culture	*wen hwah*	wén huà 文 化
cup, glass	*bay zih*	bēi zi 杯 子
currency	*hwuh bee*	huò bì 货 币
curtain	*chwahng lee-en*	chuāng lián 窗 帘
custom	*fung soo*	fēng sú 风 俗
customer	*goo kuh*	gù kè 顾 客
customs	*hye gwahn*	hǎi guān 海 关
cute	*kuh eye*	kě ài 可 爱
dad	*bah bah*	bà ba 爸 爸
daily	*may tee-en*	měi tiān 每 天
damn	*gye sih*	gāi sǐ 该 死
dance	*tee-aow woo*	tiào wǔ 跳 舞
dangerous	*way shee-en*	wēi xiǎn 危 险
dark	*hay ahn*	hēi àn 黑 暗
date (courting)	*yweh hway*	yuē huì 约 会
date (period)	*rr chee*	rì qī 日 期

daughter	*niew ar*	nǚ ér 女 儿
day	*tee-en*	tiān 天
daytime	*bye tee-en*	bái tiān 白 天
December	*Shir er yweh*	shí èr yuè 十 二 月
deep	*shen*	shēn 深
degree (college)	*shweh lee*	xué lì 学 历
degree	*doo*	dù 度
deliver	*sohng*	sòng 送
demonstrate	*yoh shing*	yóu xíng 游 行
Denmark	*Dahn mye*	Dān mài 丹 麦
dentist	*yah ee*	yá yī 牙 医
Deny	*jiew jweh*	jù jué 拒 绝
deodorant	*choo choh jee*	chú chòu jì 除 臭 剂
department	*boo men*	bù mén 部 门
depart	*choo fah*	chū fā 出 发
department store	*bye hwuh - shahng dee-en*	bǎi huò shāng diàn 百 货 商 店

deposit (money)	*yah jeen*	yā jīn 押 金
depress	*jiew sahng*	jǔ sàng 沮 丧
desk	*jwuh zih*	zhuō zi 桌 子
dessert	*tee-en dee-en*	tián diǎn 甜 点
develop (film)	*shee - jee-aow jwahn*	xǐ jiāo juǎn 洗 胶 卷
diabetes	*tahng nee-aow - bing*	táng niào bìng 糖 尿 病
diaper	*nee-aow boo*	niào bù 尿 布
diarrhea	*lah doo zih*	lā dù zi 拉 肚 子
dictionary	*zih dee-en*	zì diǎn 字 典
dining room	*tsahn ting*	cǎn tīng 餐 厅
dinner	*wahn tsahn*	wǎn cān 晚 餐
direction	*fahng shee-ahng*	fāng xiàng 方 向
dirty	*zahng*	zāng 脏
disabled person	*tsahn jee ren*	cán jí rén 残 疾 人
disaster	*zye nahn*	zāi nàn 灾 难
disco	*bung dee*	bèng dí 蹦 迪

discount	*dah juh*	dǎ zhé 打 折
dishonest	*boo chung shir*	bù cheng shí 不 诚 实
dissatisfied	*boo mahn ee*	bù mǎn yì 不 满 意
disturb	*dah raow*	dǎ rǎo 打 扰
divorce	*lee hwun*	lí hūn 离 婚
dizzy	*toh ywen*	tóu yūn 头 晕
do	*gahn*	gàn 干
doctor	*dye foo* or *ee shung*	dài fu yī shēng 大 夫 ; 医 生
dog	*goh*	gǒu 狗
doll	*yahng wah wah*	yáng wá wa 洋 娃 娃
dollar	*may ywahn*	měi yuán 美 元
domestic	*gwuh nay duh*	guó nèi de 国 内 的
door, gate	*men*	mén 门
dormitory	*soo shuh*	sù shè 宿 舍
double bed	*shwahng ren - chwahng*	shuāng rén chuáng 双 人 床
double room	*shwahng ren - fahng*	shuāng rén fáng 双 人 房

down	shee-ahng - shee-ah duh	xiàng xià de 向 下 的
downstairs	loh shee-ah	lóu xià 楼 下
downtown	shir chiew	shì qū 市 区
dozen	ee dah	yì dá 一 打
draft beer	jah pee	zhā pí 扎 啤
dragon	lohng	lóng 龙
dress (noun)	lee-en ee chwun	lián yī qún 连 衣 裙
dress (verb)	chwahn	chuān 穿
drink (verb)	huh	hē 喝
drinks (noun)	jeo shway	jiǔ shuǐ 酒 水
drive (car)	kye chuh	kāi chē 开 (车)
driver	sih jee	sī jī 司 机
driver's license	jee-ah shir - jir jaow	jià shǐ zhí zhào 驾 驶 执 照
drop (verb)	lwuh shee-ah	luò xià 落 下
drug (medicine)	yaow	yào 药
drug (poison)	doo peen	dú pǐn 毒 品

drugstore	*yaow dee-en*	yào diàn 药 店
drunk, tipsy	*huh zway luh*	hē zuì le 喝 醉 了
dry cleaner's	*gahn shee - dee-en*	gàn xǐ diàn 干 洗 店
dry	*gahn*	gān 干
dry-clean	*gahn shee*	gàn xǐ 干 洗
duck	*yah zih*	yā zi 鸭 子
dull, dim, dark	*yeen ahn*	yīn àn 阴 暗
dust (noun)	*hway chen*	huī chén 灰 尘
each	*may ee guh*	měi yí gè 每 一 个
ear	*ar dwuh*	ěr duo 耳 朵
earache	*ar dwuh tung*	ěr duo téng 耳 朵 疼
early	*zaow duh*	zǎo de 早 的
earring	*ar hwahn*	ěr huán 耳 环
earth (planet)	*dee cheo*	dì qiú 地 球
earthquake	*dee jen*	dì zhèn 地 震
easiest	*zway rohng ee - duh*	zuì róng yì de 最 容 易 的

east	***dohng fahng***	dōng fāng 东 方
easy	***rohng ee***	róng yì 容 易
eat	***chir***	chī 吃
economy	***jing jee***	jīng jì 经 济
education	***jee-aow yiew***	jiào yù 教 育
effective	***yoh shee-aow - duh***	yǒu xiào de 有 效 的
egg	***jee dahn***	jī dàn 鸡 蛋
eggplant	***chee-eh zih***	qié zi 茄 子
Egypt	***Eye jee***	Ai jí 埃 及
eight	***bah***	bā 八
eighteen	***shir bah***	shí bā 十 八
eighth	***dee bah guh***	dì bā gè 第 八 个
electric plug	***dee-en chah toh***	diàn chā tóu 电 插 头
electricity	***dee-en***	diàn 电
elevator	***dee-en tee***	diàn tī 电 梯
eleven	***shir ee***	shí yī 十 一

email	*dee-en zih yoh - jee-en*	diàn zǐ yóu jiàn 电 子 邮 件
embassy	*dah shir gwahn*	dà shǐ guǎn 大 使 馆
emergency room	*jee jeo shir*	jí jiù shì 急 救 室
emergency	*jeen jee - ching kwahng*	jǐn jí qíng kuàng 紧 急 情 况
employee	*goo ywahn*	gù yuán 雇 员
empty	*kohng duh*	kōng de 空 的
energy	*nung lee-ahng*	néng liàng 能 量
engineer	*gohng chung - shir*	gōng chéng shī 工 程 师
England	*Ying gwuh*	Yīng guó 英 国
English (people)	*Ying gwuh ren*	Yīng guó rén 英 国 人
English language	*Ying yiew*	yīng yǔ 英 语
enjoy	*shee eye*	xǐ ài 喜 爱
enough	*goh luh*	gòu le 够 了
enterprise	*chee yee-eh*	qǐ yè 企 业
entire, whole	*jung guh*	zhěng gè 整 个
entrance	*roo koh*	rù kǒu 入 口

entry visa	*roo jing - chee-en jung*	rù jìng qiān zhèng 入境 签 证
envelope	*sheen fung*	xìn fēng 信 封
environment	*hwahn jing*	huán jìng 环 境
error	*tswuh woo*	cuò wù 错 误
escalator	*zih dohng - foo tee*	zì dòng fú tī 自 动 扶 梯
Europe	*Oh joh*	Ou zhōu 欧 洲
European (people)	*Oh joh ren*	Ou zhōu rén 欧 洲 人
even (number)	*oh shoo*	ǒu shù 偶 数
even (fair)	*gohng ping*	gōng píng 公 平
evening	*wahn shahng*	wǎn shang 晚 上
everyday	*may tee-en*	měi tiān 每 天
examination	*kaow shir*	kǎo shì 考 试
example	*lee zih*	lì zi 例 子
except	*choo luh*	chú le 除 了
exchange rate	*hway liew*	huì lǜ 汇 率
excuse	*jee-eh koh*	jiè kǒu 借 口

exercise	*dwahn lee-en*	duàn liàn 锻 炼
exhausted	*pee bay*	pí bèi 疲 惫
exit visa	*choo jing -*	chū jìng 出 境
	chee-en jung	qiān zhèng 签 证
exit	*choo koh*	chū kǒu 出 口
expensive	*gway*	guì 贵
export (verb)	*choo koh*	chū kǒu 出 口
express (verb)	*bee-aow dah*	biǎo dá 表 达
express letter	*tuh kwye -* *jwahn dee*	tè kuài zhuān dì 特 快 专 递
express train	*tuh kwye -* *lee-eh chuh*	tè kuài liè chē 特 快 列 车
expression	*bee-aow ching*	biǎo qíng 表 情
extension cord	*jee-eh shee-en -* *bahn*	jiē xiàn bǎn 接 线 板
extra	*uh wye duh*	é wài de 额 外 的
eye drops	*yee-en yaow -* *shway*	yǎn yào shuǐ 眼 药 水
eye	*yee-en jing*	yǎn jīng 眼 睛
face	*lee-en*	liǎn 脸

191

fact	*shir shir*	shì shí 事 实
factory	*gohng chahng*	gōng chǎng 工 厂
fahrenheit	*Hwah shir doo*	huá shì dù 华 氏 度
fail	*shir bye*	shī bài 失 败
faint	*ywin daow*	yūn dǎo 晕 倒
faint (adj.)	*shiew rwuh duh*	xū ruò de 虚 弱 的
fake (adj.)	*jee-ah duh*	jiǎ de 假 的
fall (verb)	*lwuh shee-ah*	luò xià 落 下
family	*jee-ah ting*	jiā tíng 家 庭
famine	*jee hwahng*	jī huāng 饥 荒
famous	*joo ming duh*	zhù míng de 著 名 的
fan (electric)	*dee-en shahn*	diàn shàn 电 扇
far	*ywahn*	yuǎn 远
fart	*fahng pee*	fàng pì 放 屁
fashion	*shir jwahng*	shí zhuāng 时 装
fast	*kwye*	kuài 快

fast food	*kwye tsahn*	kuài cān 快 餐
fat	*pahng*	pàng 胖
father	*gung ywahn*	gèng yuǎn 更 远
fault	*gwuh tswuh*	guò cuò 过 错
fax	*dee-en baow*	diàn bào 电 报
fear	*dahn sheen*	dān xīn 担 心
February	*Ar yweh*	èr yuè 二 月
fee, expense	*fay yohng*	fèi yòng 费 用
feel	*gahn jweh*	gǎn jué 感 觉
female	*niew duh*	nǚ de 女 的
ferry	*doo chwahn*	dù chuán 渡 船
festival	*jee-eh rr*	jié rì 节 日
fever	*fah shaow*	fā shāo 发 烧
few	*jee guh*	jǐ gè 几 个
fiancé	*way hwun foo*	wèi hūn fū 未 婚 夫
fifteen	*shir woo*	shí wǔ 十 五

fifth	*dee woo guh*	dì wǔ gè 第五个
fight	*dah jee-ah*	dǎ jià 打架
film (camera)	*jee-aow jwahn*	jiāo juǎn 胶卷
film (movie)	*dee-en ying*	diàn yǐng 电影
find	*jaow daow*	zhǎo dào 找到
fine	*haow*	hǎo 好
fine, penalty	*fah kwahn*	fá kuǎn 罚款
finger	*shoh jir*	shǒu zhǐ 手指
Finland	*Fen lahn*	Fēn lán 芬兰
fire alarm	*hwuh jing*	huǒ jǐng 火警
fire	*hwuh*	huǒ 火
firecracker	*bee-en paow*	biān pào 鞭炮
first class (flight)	*toh dung tsahng*	tóu děng cāng 头等舱
first	*dee ee (guh)*	dì yī gè 第一（个）
first-aid kit	*jee jeo - shee-ahng*	jí jiù xiāng 急救箱
fish	*yiew*	yú 鱼

fisherman	*yiew meen*	yú mín 渔 民
five	*woo*	wǔ 五
flash (camera)	*shahn gwahng - dung*	shǎn guāng dēng 闪 光 灯
flashlight	*shoh dee-en - tohng*	shǒu diàn tǒng 手 电 筒
flavor	*zih way*	zī wèi 滋 味
flight	*hahng bahn*	háng bān 航 班
flood	*hohng shway*	hóng shuǐ 洪 水
floor	*dee bahn*	dì bǎn 地 板
flower	*hwah*	huā 花
flu	*leo gahn*	liú gǎn 流 感
fluency	*leo lee*	liú lì 流 利
fly (insect)	*tsahng ying*	cāng ying 苍 蝇
fly (verb)	*fay*	fēi 飞
fog	*woo*	wù 雾
foggy	*woo hung dah*	wù hěn dà 雾 很 大
food poisoning	*shir woo johng - doo*	shí wù zhòng dú 食 物 中 毒

195

food	**shir woo**	shí wù 食 物	
foot (body part)	**jee-aow**	jiǎo 脚	
football (soccer)	**zoo cheo**	zú qiú 足 球	
football (U.S.)	**gahn lahn cheo**	gǎn lǎn qiú 橄 榄 球	
for	**way luh**	wèi le 为 了	
foreign	**wye gwuh duh**	wài guó de 外 国 的	
Foreign Affairs Branch	**Wye shir kuh**	wài shì kē 外 事 科	
foreign exchange	**wye hway**	wài huì 外 汇	
foreigner	**wye gwuh ren**	wài guó rén 外 国 人	
forest	**sen leen**	sēn lín 森 林	
forget	**wahng jee**	wàng jì 忘 记	
fork	**chah zih**	chā zi 叉 子	
form (noun)	**bee-aow**	biǎo 表	
form (verb)	**shing chung**	xíng chéng 形 成	
formal	**jung shir duh**	zhèng shì de 正 式 的	
four	**sih**	sì 四	

English	Pronunciation	Chinese
fourteen	*shir sih*	shí sì 十 四
fourth	*dee sih guh*	dì sì gè 第 四 个
France	*Fah gwuh*	Fǎ guó 法 国
free (cost)	*mee-en fay duh*	miǎn fèi de 免 费 的
free (time)	*yoh shir jee-en*	yǒu shí jiān 有 时 间
freezing	*bing lung duh*	bīng lěng de 冰 冷 的
French language	*Fah yiew*	Fǎ yǔ 法 语
fresh	*sheen shee-en - duh*	xīn xiān de 新 鲜 的
Friday	*Shing chee woo*	xīng qī wǔ 星 期 五
fried	*chaow duh*	chǎo de 炒 的
friend	*pung yoh*	péng you 朋 友
friendly	*yoh haow duh*	yǒu hǎo de 友 好 地
friendship	*yoh ee*	yǒu yì 友 谊
from	*tsohng...*	cóng 从 …
front desk	*chee-en tye*	qián tái 前 台
frost	*shwahng*	shuāng 霜

197

fruit	**shway gwuh**	shuǐ guǒ 水果
fuck (verb)	**shing jee-aow**	xìng jiāo 性交
Fuck!	**Tsaow!**	Cào 操！
full	**mahn duh** or	mǎn de 满的；
	chwahn boo duh	quán bù de 全部的
fun	**yoh chiew duh**	yǒu qù de 有趣的
furniture	**jee-ah jiew**	jiā jù 家具
fuse (noun)	**baow shee-en - sih**	bǎo xiǎn sī 保险丝
future	**jee-ahng lye**	jiāng lái 将来
gallon	**jee-ah lwun**	jiā lún 加仑
gamble	**doo bwuh**	dǔ bó 赌博
game	**bee sye**	bǐ sài 比赛
garage	**chuh koo**	chē kù 车库
garbage	**lah jee**	lā jī 垃圾
garden	**hwah ywahn**	huā yuán 花园
garlic	**swahn**	suàn 蒜

gas station	*jee-ah yoh jahn*	jiā yóu zhàn 加 油 站
gasoline	*chee yoh*	qì yóu 汽 油
gate	*dah men*	dà mén 大 门
generous	*kahng kye duh*	kāng kǎi de 慷 慨 的
genuine	*chung ken duh*	chéng kěn de 诚 恳 的
German	*Duh gwuh*	Dé guó 德 国
German (people)	*Duh gwuh ren*	Dé guó rén 德 国 人
get on (to board)	*shahng*	shàng 上
get up	*chee lye*	qǐ lái 起 来
gift	*lee woo*	lǐ wù 礼 物
ginger	*jee-ahng*	jiāng 姜
ginseng	*ren shen*	rén shēn 人 参
girl	*niew har*	nǚ hái ér 女 孩 儿
girlfriend	*niew pung yoh*	nǚ péng you 女 朋 友
give	*gay*	gěi 给
glass	*bwuh lee*	bō li 玻 璃

199

glasses (optical)	*yahn jing*	yǎn jìng 眼 镜
gloves	*shoh taow*	shǒu tào 手 套
go	*chiew* or *zoh*	qù　　zǒu 去 ; 走
goat	*shahn yahng*	shān yáng 山 羊
gold	*jeen zih*	jīn zi 金 子
goldfish	*jeen yiew*	jīn yú 金 鱼
golf	*gaow ar foo - cheo*	gāo ěr fū qiú 高 尔 夫 球
good	*haow*	hǎo 好
Good-bye.	*Zye jee-en.*	Zài jiàn 再 见 。
government	*jung foo*	zhèng fǔ 政 府
gracious	*gaow shahng - duh*	gāo shàng de 高 尚 的
gram	*kuh*	kè 克
grammar	*yiew fah*	yǔ fǎ 语 法
grandfather (matriarchal)	*laow yee-eh*	lǎo ye 老 爷
grandfather (patriarchal)	*yee-eh yee-eh*	yé ye 爷 爷
grandmother (matriarchal)	*laow laow*	lǎo lao 姥 姥

English	Pronunciation	Pinyin	Chinese
grandmother (patriarchal)	*nye nye*	nǎi nai	奶奶
grape juice	*poo taow jir*	pú tao zhī	葡萄汁
grape	*poo taow*	pú tao	葡萄
greasy	*yoh nee duh*	yóu nì de	油腻的
Great Wall	*Chahng chung*	cháng chéng	长城
great	*way dah*	wěi dà	伟大
Great!	*Tye bahng luh!*	Tài bàng le	太棒了！
Greece	*Shee lah*	Xī là	希腊
green pepper	*ching jee-aow*	qīng jiāo	青椒
green tea	*liew chah*	lǜ chá	绿茶
grocery store	*zah hwuh dee-en*	zá huò diàn	杂货店
grocery	*zah hwuh*	zá huò	杂货
ground	*dee mee-en*	dì miàn	地面
group	*twahn*	tuán	团
Guangzhou	*Gwahng joh*	Guǎng zhōu	广州
guarantee	*baow jung*	bǎo zhèng	保证

guest	**kuh ren**	kè rén 客人
guide (person)	**daow yoh**	dǎo yóu 导游
guidebook	**liew shing - jir nahn**	lǚ xíng zhǐ nán 旅行指南
gum	**koh shee-ahng - tahng**	kǒu xiāng táng 口香糖
gymnasium	**jee-en shen - fahng**	jiàn shēn fáng 健身房
gynecologist	**foo kuh - ee shung**	fù kē yī shēng 妇科医生
habit	**shee gwahn**	xí guàn 习惯
hair	**toh fah**	tóu fà 头发
haircut	**lee fah**	lǐ fà 理发
hairdresser	**lee fah shir**	lǐ fà shī 理发师
half	**ee bahn**	yí bàn 一半
ham	**hwuh tway**	huǒ tuǐ 火腿
hand towel	**shoh jeen**	shǒu jīn 手巾
hand	**shoh**	shǒu 手
handbag	**shoh tee baow**	shǒu tí bāo 手提包
handicapped	**tsahn jee ren**	cán jí rén 残疾人

handicraft	***shoh gohng ee - peen***	shǒu gōng yì pǐn 手 工 艺 品
handsome	***ying jwin***	yīng jùn 英 俊
hanger	***ee foo jee-ah***	yī fu jià 衣 服 架
happy	***gaow shing***	gāo xìng 高 兴
harbor	***gahng koh***	gǎng kǒu 港 口
hard (difficult)	***kwun nahn duh***	kùn nan de 困 难 的
hard (rigid)	***ying***	yìng 硬
has (to have)	***yoh***	yǒu 有
hat	***maow zih***	mào zi 帽 子
have	***yoh***	yǒu 有
hay fever	***hwah fen ruh***	huā fěn rè 花 粉 热
he	***tah***	tā 他
head	***toh***	tóu 头
headache	***toh tung***	tóu téng 头 疼
health	***jee-en kahng***	jiàn kāng 健 康
healthy	***jee-en kahng - duh***	jiàn kāng de 健 康 的

heart attack	***sheen zahng - bing fah zwuh***	^{xīn} 心 ^{zàng} 脏 ^{bìng} 病 ^{fā} 发 ^{zuò} 作
heart	***sheen***	xīn 心
heater	***nwahn chee***	nuǎn qì 暖 气
heating	***jee-ah ruh***	jiā rè 加 热
heavy	***johng***	zhòng 重
hello (greeting on phone)	***way***	wéi 喂
hello	***nee haow***	nǐ hǎo 你 好
help	***bahng joo*** or ***bahng mahng***	bāng zhù 帮 助；bāng máng 帮 忙
her	***tah***	tā 她
here	***juh***	zhè 这
hers	***tah duh***	tā de 她 的
high school	***gaow johng***	gāo zhōng 高 中
high, tall	***gaow***	gāo 高
highway	***gaow soo - gohng loo***	gāo sù gōng lù 高 速 公 路

hike	*ywahn zoo*	yuǎn zú 远 足
hill	*shee-aow shahn*	xiǎo shān 小 山
him	*tah*	tā 他
hire (someone)	*goo yohng*	gù yòng 雇 用
his	*tah duh*	tā de 他 的
history	*lee shir*	lì shǐ 历 史
hobby	*eye haow*	ài hào 爱 好
holiday	*jee-ah chee*	jià qī 假 期
home	*jee-ah*	jiā 家
homesick	*shee-ahng jee-ah*	xiǎng jiā 想 家
hometown	*jee-ah shee-ahng*	jiā xiāng 家 乡
homosexual	*tohng shing - lee-en*	tóng xìng liàn 同 性 恋
honest	*chung shir*	chéng shí 诚 实
Honey (title of endearment)	*Cheen eye duh*	qīn ài de 亲 爱 的
honey	*fung mee*	fēng mì 蜂 蜜

Hong Kong	*Shee-ahng - gahng*	Xiāng gǎng 香 港
horse	*mah*	mǎ 马
hospital	*ee ywahn*	yī yuàn 医 院
hospitality	*shung ching*	shèng qíng 盛 情
hot water	*ruh shway*	rè shuǐ 热 水
hot	*ruh*	rè 热
hotel / restaurant	*fahn dee-en*	fàn diàn 饭 店
hotel	*liew gwahn* or *jeo dee-en*	lǚ guǎn ; jiǔ diàn 旅 馆 ; 酒 店
hour	*shee-aow shir*	xiǎo shí 小 时
house	*fahng zih*	fáng zi 房 子
how	*zen muh*	zěn me 怎 么
humorous	*yoh mwuh*	yōu mò 幽 默
hungry	*uh*	è 饿
hurry	*gahn jeen*	gǎn jǐn 赶 紧
hurt (verb)	*shahng hye*	shāng hài 伤 害
husband	*jahng foo*	zhàng fu 丈 夫

I, me	**wuh**	wǒ 我
ice cream	**bing chee leen**	bīng qí lín 冰 淇 淋
ice skating	**hwah bing**	huá bīng 滑 冰
ice water	**bing shway**	bīng shuǐ 冰 水
Ice	**blng**	bīng 冰
icy	**bing lung duh**	bīng lěng de 冰 冷 的
idiom	**chung yiew**	chéng yǔ 成 语
idiot	**bye chir**	bái chī 白 痴
if	**jee-ah roo**	jiǎ rú 假 如
ill, sick	**bing luh**	bìng le 病 了
illegal	**fay fah duh**	fēi fǎ de 非 法 的
immediately	**mah shahng**	mǎ shàng 马 上
immigration	**ee meen**	yí mín 移 民
import (item)	**jeen koh**	jìn kǒu 进 口
important	**johng yaow**	zhòng yào 重 要
impossible	**boo kuh nung - duh**	bù kě néng de 不 可 能 的

in front of ___	**zye___chee-en - mee-en**	zài qián mian 在 ___ 前 面
income tax	**swuh duh shway**	suǒ dé shuì 所 得 税
income	**shoh roo**	shōu rù 收 入
India	**Yeen doo**	Yìn dù 印 度
indigestion	**shee-aow hwah - boo lee-ahng**	xiāo huà bù liáng 消 化 不 良
indoor	**shir nay**	shì nèi 室 内
industry	**gohng yeh**	gōng yè 工 业
inexpensive	**boo gway**	bú guì 不 贵
infected	**gahn rahn luh**	gǎn rǎn le 感 染 了
information	**sheen shee**	xìn xī 信 息
information desk	**wen shwin choo**	wèn xún chù 问 询 处
inject	**joo shuh**	zhù shè 注 射
injured	**shoh shahng luh**	shòu shāng le 受 伤 了
Inner Mongolia	**Nay mung goo**	Nèi měng gǔ 内 蒙 古
insect repellant	**chiew chohng - jee**	qū chóng jì 驱 虫 剂
inside	**lee mee-en**	lǐ miàn 里 面

insurance	***baow shee-en***	bǎo xiǎn 保 险
intelligent	***tsohng ming***	cōng ming 聪 明
interest (money)	***lee shee***	lì xi 利 息
interest rate	***lee liew***	lì lù 利 率
Interesting	***yoh ee sih***	yǒu yì si 有 意 思
international	***gwuh jee duh***	guó jì de 国 际 的
internet	***yeen tuh wahng***	yīn tè wǎng 囚 特 网
interpreter	***fahn ee***	fān yì 翻 译
intersection	***shir zih loo koh***	shí zì lù kǒu 十 字 路 口
introduce	***jee-eh shaow***	jiè shào 介 绍
invest	***toh zih***	tóu zī 投 资
invite	***yaow ching***	yāo qǐng 邀 请
Iran	***Ee lahng***	Yī lǎng 伊 朗
Iraq	***Ee lah kuh***	Yī lā kè 伊 拉 克
Ireland	***Eye ar lahn***	Ai ěr lán 爱 尔 兰

iron (for ironing clothes)	***dee-en ywin - doh***	diàn yùn dǒu 电 熨 斗
iron (verb)	***ywin ee foo***	yùn yī fu 熨 衣 服
irrigate (a cut)	***chohng shee - (shahng koh)***	chōng xǐ 冲 洗 shāng kǒu （伤 口）
is	***shir***	shì 是
island	***daow***	dǎo 岛
it	***tah***	tā 它
Italy	***Ee dah lee***	Yì dà lì 意 大 利
jacket	***jee-ah kuh shahn***	jiá kè shān 夹 克 衫
jade	***yiew***	yù 玉
jail, prison	***jee-en yiew***	jiān yù 监 狱
January	***Ee yweh***	yī yuè 一 月
Japan	***Rr ben***	Rì běn 日 本
jazz	***jweh shir yweh***	jué shì yuè 爵 士 乐
jeans	***niew zye koo***	niú zǎi kù 牛 仔 裤

jeep	*jee poo chuh*	jí pǔ chē 吉普车
jewelry	*shoh shir*	shǒu shì 首饰
job	*gohng zwuh*	gōng zuò 工作
joke (noun)	*shee-aow hwah*	xiào huà 笑话
joking	*kye wahn - shee-aow*	kāi wán xiào 开玩笑
journalist	*jee juh*	jì zhě 记者
journey	*liew shing*	lǚ xíng 旅行
judo	*roh daow*	róu dào 柔道
juice	*gwuh jir*	guǒ zhī 果汁
July	*Chee yiew*	qī yuè 七月
June	*Leo yiew*	liù yuè 六月
just	*jir shir*	zhǐ shì 只是
justice	*jung ee*	zhèng yì 正义
Karachi	*Kah lah chee*	Kǎ lā qí 卡拉奇
karaoke	*kah lah okay*	kǎ lā 卡拉 O K
karate	*kohng shoh - daow*	kōng shǒu dào 空手道

kettle, pot	*hoo*	hú 壶
key	*yaow shir*	yào shi 钥 匙
kilogram	*gohng jeen*	gōng jīn 公 斤
kilometer	*gohng lee*	gōng li 公 里
kindergarten	*yoh er ywahn*	yòu ér yuán 幼 儿 园
kiss	*wen*	wěn 吻
kitchen	*choo fahng*	chú fáng 厨 房
kite	*fung jung*	fēng zhēng 风 筝
Kleenex	*mee-en jeen jir*	miàn jīn zhǐ 面 巾 纸
knee	*shee gye*	xī gài 膝 盖
knife	*daow*	dāo 刀
knit	*bee-en jir*	biān zhī 编 织
knot	*dah jee-eh*	dǎ jié 打 结
know	*jir daow*	zhī dào 知 道
know sb. well	*lee-aow jee-eh*	liǎo jiě 了 解
Korea	*Hahn gwuh*	Hán guó 韩 国

Kuwait	*Kuh way tuh*	Kē wēi tè 科 威 特
label (noun)	*bee-aow chee-en*	biāo qiān 标 签
labor work	*tee lee gohng - zwuh*	tǐ lì gōng zuò 体 力 工 作
laboratory	*shir yahn shir*	shí yàn shì 实 验 室
lake	*hoo*	hú 湖
lamb	*yahng gaow*	yáng gāo 羊 羔
lamp	*dung*	dēng 灯
landlord	*fahng dohng*	fáng dōng 房 东
language	*yiew yahn*	yǔ yán 语 言
Lantern Festival	*Ywahn shee-aow- jee-eh*	Yuán xiāo jié 元 宵 节
Los Angeles	*Lwuh shahn jee*	Luò shān jī 洛 杉 矶
last (verb)	*chir shiew*	chí xù 持 续
last	*zway hoh*	zuì hòu 最 后
late	*wahn luh*	wǎn le 晚 了
later	*sway hoh*	suí hòu 随 后
laugh	*shee-aow*	xiào 笑

laundry (clothing)	*shee ee foo*	xǐ yī fu 洗衣服
law	*fah liew*	fǎ lù 法律
lawyer	*liew shir*	lù shī 律师
lazy	*lahn dwuh*	lǎn duò 懒惰
learn	*shweh shee*	xué xí 学习
leather	*pee guh*	pí gé 皮革
leave (depart)	*lee kye*	lí kāi 离开
leave a message	*leo yahn*	liú yán 留言
lecture	*yahn jee-ahng*	yǎn jiǎng 演讲
left side	*zwuh bee-en*	zuǒ biān 左边
leg	*tway*	tuǐ 腿
legal	*huh fah duh*	hé fǎ de 合法的
lemon	*ning mung*	níng méng 柠檬
lemonade	*ning mung - shway*	níng méng shuǐ 柠檬水
lend	*jee-eh gay*	jiè gěi 借给
lenient	*ren tsih duh*	rén cí de 仁慈的

lens (camera)	*jing toh*	jìng tóu 镜 头
letter	*sheen*	xìn 信
lettuce	*shung tsye*	shēng cài 生 菜
Lhasa	*Lah sah*	Lā sà 拉 萨
library	*too shoo gwahn*	tú shū guǎn 图 书 馆
license	*jir jaow*	zhí zhào 执 照
lichee	*lee jir*	lì zhī 荔 枝
lid	*gye zih*	gài zi 盖 子
light	*dung*	dēng 灯
lighter (adjective)	*ching duh*	qīng de 轻 的
lighter (noun)	*dah hwuh jee*	dǎ huǒ jī 打 火 机
lightning	*shahn dee-en*	shǎn diàn 闪 电
like (verb)	*shee hwahn*	xǐ huān 喜 欢
lips	*zway chwun*	zuǐ chún 嘴 唇
lipstick	*chwun gaow*	chún gāo 唇 膏
liquor	*jeo shway*	jiǔ shuǐ 酒 水

liter	*gohng shung*	gōng shēng 公 升
literature	*wen shweh*	wén xué 文 学
little	*shee-aow*	xiǎo 小
a little (amount)	*ee dee-en*	yì diǎn 一 点
live	*joo zye*	zhù zài 住 在
live band	*shee-en chahng-*	xiàn chǎng 现 场
	yweh dway	yuè duì 乐 队
liver	*gahn zahng*	gān zàng 肝 脏
living room	*kuh ting*	kè tīng 客 厅
lobby	*dah ting*	dà tīng 大 厅
lobster	*lohng shee-ah*	lóng xiā 龙 虾
lock (noun)	*swuh*	suǒ 锁
lock (verb)	*swuh shahng*	suǒ shàng 锁 上
London	*Lwen dwun*	Lún dūn 伦 敦
long	*chahng duh*	cháng de 长 的
long-distance	*ywahn jiew lee - duh*	yuǎn jù lí de 远 距 离 的

longer	**gung ywahn duh** or **gung chahng - duh**	gèng yuǎn de 更 远 的 ; gèng cháng de 更 长 的
look	**kahn**	kàn 看
lose face	**deo lee-en**	diū liǎn 丢 脸
lose	**deo**	diū 丢
lose a game	**shoo luh**	shū le 输 了
lost and found	**shir woo jaow - ling**	shī wù zhe lǐng 失 物 招 领
loud	**dah shung duh**	dà shēng de 大 声 的
love	**eye**	ài 爱
lover	**eye ren**	ài rén 爱 人
luck	**ywen chee**	yùn qì 运 气
luggage	**shing lee**	xíng li 行 李
lunar calendar	**yeen lee**	yīn lì 阴 历
lunch	**woo fahn**	wǔ fàn 午 饭
lung	**fay**	fèi 肺
Macao	**Aow men**	Ao mén 澳 门

English	Pronunciation	Chinese
machine	*jee chee*	jī qì 机 器
Madrid	*Mah duh lee*	Mǎ dé lǐ 马 德 里
magazine	*zah jir*	zá zhì 杂 志
magician	*mwuh shoo shir*	mó shù shī 魔 术 师
mahjong	*mah jee-ahng*	má jiàng 麻 将
mail (noun)	*sheen*	xìn 信
mail (verb)	*jee*	jì 寄
mainland	*dah loo*	dà lù 大 陆
make	*zwuh*	zuò 做
makeup (noun)	*hwah jwahng - peen*	huà zhuāng pǐn 化 妆 品
makeup (verb)	*hwah jwahng*	huà zhuāng 化 妆
Malaysia	*Mah lah shee - yah*	Mǎ lái xī yà 马 来 西 亚
male	*nahn shing*	nán xìng 男 性
man	*nahn ren*	nán rén 男 人
manage	*gwahn lee*	guǎn lǐ 管 理
manager	*jing lee*	jīng lǐ 经 理

Mandarin	*Poo tohng hwah*	pǔ tōng huà 普 通 话
mango	*mahng gwuh*	máng guǒ 芒 果
Manila	*Mah nee lah*	Mǎ ní lā 马 尼 拉
man-made	*ren zaow duh*	rén zào de 人 造 的
manufacture	*jee-ah gohng*	jiā gōng 加 工
many	*hen dwuh*	hěn duō 很 多
Mao Zedong	*Maow - Zuh dohng*	Máo zé dōng 毛 泽 东
map	*dee too*	de tú 地 图
March	*Sahn yweh*	sān yuè 三 月
mark	*bee-aow jir*	biǎo zhì 标 志
market	*shir chahng*	shì chǎng 市 场
marketing	*ying shee-aow*	yíng xiāo 营 销
married	*ee hwun duh*	yǐ hūn de 已 婚 的
marry	*jee-eh hwun*	jié hūn 结 婚
martial arts	*woo shoo*	wǔ shù 武 术
mask	*mee-en jiew*	miàn jù 面 具

219

medical mask	**koh jaow**	kǒu zhào 口 罩
massage	**ahn mwuh**	àn mó 按 摩
master	**dah shir** or **shir foo**	dà shī shī fu 大 师 ; 师 傅
matches	**hwuh chye**	huǒ chái 火 柴
matter	**shir jee-en**	shì jiàn 事 件
mattress	**chwahng dee-en**	chuáng diàn 床 垫
May	**Woo yweh**	wǔ yuè 五 月
maybe	**yee-eh shiew**	yě xǔ 也 许
me	**wuh**	wǒ 我
meal	**ee dwun fahn**	yí dùn fàn 一 顿 饭
measure (verb)	**lee-ahng**	liáng 量
meat	**roh**	ròu 肉
mechanic	**jee shee-eh - gohng ren**	jī xiè gōng rén 机 械 工 人
medicine	**yaow**	yào 药
medium (size)	**johng haow duh**	zhōng hào de 中 号 的
meet	**yiew___jee-en - mee-en**	yǔ jiàn miàn 与___见 面

meeting	*hway ee*	huì yì 会 议
Melbourne	*Muh ar ben*	Mò ěr běn 墨 尔 本
melon	*gwah*	guā 瓜
menu	*tsye dahn*	cài dān 菜 单
merry	*ylew kwye duh*	yú kuài de 愉 快 的
message	*shee-aow shee*	xiāo xi 消 息
metal	*jeen shoo*	jīn shǔ 金 属
meter (distance)	*mee*	mǐ 米
meter (taxi)	*bee-aow*	biǎo 表
Mexico	*Mwuh shee guh*	Mò xī gē 墨 西 哥
microphone	*mye kuh fung*	mài kè fēng 麦 克 风
middle	*johng jee-en*	zhōng jiān 中 间
midnight	*woo yee-eh*	wǔ yè 午 夜
military	*jwin shir duh*	jūn shì de 军 事 的
milk	*neo nye*	niú nǎi 牛 奶
million	*bye wahn*	bǎi wàn 百 万

mine	*wuh duh*	wǒ de 我 的
mineral water	*kwahng chwahn-shway*	kuàng quán shuǐ 矿 泉 水
minority (people)	*shaow shoo - meen zoo*	shǎo shù mín zú 少 数 民 族
minute	*fen johng*	fēn zhōng 分 钟
mirror	*jing zih*	jìng zi 镜 子
mistake	*tswuh woo*	cuò wù 错 误
mobile phone	*shoh jee*	shǒu jī 手 机
model (person)	*mwuh tuh*	mó tè 模 特
modest	*chee-en shiew*	qiān xū 谦 虚
Monday	*Shing chee ee*	xīng qī yī 星 期 一
money order	*hway pee-aow*	huì piào 汇 票
money	*chee-en*	qián 钱
Mongolia	*Mung goo*	Měng gǔ 蒙 古
monk	*huh shahng*	hé shang 和 尚
monkey	*hoh zih*	hóu zi 猴 子
month	*yiew*	yuè 月

Montreal	*Mung tuh lee ar*	Měng tè lì ěr 蒙 特 利 尔
monument	*jee nee-en bay*	jì niàn bēi 纪 念 碑
moon	*yweh lee-ahng*	yuè liàng 月 亮
moral	*yoh daow duh - duh*	yǒu dào dé de 有 道 德 的
more	*gung dwuh duh*	gèng duō de 更 多 的
morning	*zaow shahng*	zǎo shang 早 上
Moscow	*Mwuh sih kuh*	Mò sī kē 莫 斯 科
Moslem	*Moo sih leen*	Mù sī lín 穆 斯 林
mosquito	*wen zih*	wén zi 蚊 子
most of	*dah dwuh shoo - duh*	dà duō shù de 大 多 数 的
mother	*moo cheen*	mǔ qīn 母 亲
motorbike	*mwuh twuh chuh*	mó tuō chē 摩 托 车
mountain	*shahn*	shān 山
mouth	*zway*	zuǐ 嘴
movie theater	*dee-en ying - ywahn*	diàn yǐng yuàn 电 影 院
movie	*dee-en ying*	diàn yǐng 电 影

MSG	*way jing*	wèi jīng 味 精
much	*hen dwuh*	hěn duō 很 多
muscles	*jee roh*	jī ròu 肌 肉
museum	*bwuh woo - gwahn*	bó wù guǎn 博 物 馆
mushroom	*mwuh goo*	mó gu 蘑 菇
music	*yeen yweh*	yīn yuè 音 乐
musical instrument	*yweh chee*	yuè qì 乐 器
muskmelon	*shee-ahng gwah*	xiāng guā 香 瓜
mustard	*jee-eh mwuh*	jiè mo 芥 末
mutton	*yahng roh*	yáng ròu 羊 肉
my	*wuh duh*	wǒ de 我 的
myself	*wuh zih jee*	wǒ zì jǐ 我 自 己
nail	*ding zih*	dīng zi 钉 子
nail (finger nail)	*jir jee-ah*	zhǐ jia 指 甲
nail clippers	*jir jee-ah daow*	zhǐ jiǎ dāo 指 甲 刀
name	*ming zih*	míng zi 名 字

nap	*shee-aow shway*	xiǎo shuì 小 睡
napkin	*tsahn jeen jir*	cān jīn zhǐ 餐 巾 纸
narrow, cramped	*shee-ah jye duh*	xiá zhǎi de 狭 窄 的
nation	*gwuh jee-ah*	guó jiā 国 家
national anthem	*gwuh guh*	guó gē 国 歌
national flag	*gwuh chee*	guó qí 国 旗
nationality	*gwuh jee*	guó jí 国 籍
navy	*hye jwin*	hǎi jūn 海 军
near	*zye ___ foo jeen*	zài fù jìn 在___附 近
neck	*bwuh zih*	bó zi 脖 子
necklace	*shee-ahng - lee-en*	xiàng liàn 项 链
necktie	*ling dye*	lǐng dài 领 带
need	*shiew yaow*	xū yào 需 要
needle	*jen*	zhēn 针
negative (film)	*dee pee-en*	dǐ piàn 底 片
negative	*foh ding duh*	fǒu dìng de 否 定 的

neighbor	*leen jiew*	lín jū 邻 居
Netherlands	*Huh lahn*	Hé lán 荷 兰
never	*tsohng boo*	cóng bù 从 不
New Year	*Sheen nee-en*	xīn nián 新 年
New York	*Neo yweh*	Niǔ yuē 纽 约
New Zealand	*Sheen shee lahn*	Xīn xī lán 新 西 兰
new	*sheen duh*	xīn de 新 的
news	*sheen wen*	xīn wén 新 闻
newspaper	*baow jir*	bào zhǐ 报 纸
next week	*shee-ah guh - shing chee*	xià gè xīng qī 下 个 星 期
next	*shee-ah ee guh*	xià yí gè 下 一 个
nice	*haow*	hǎo 好
night	*wahn shahng*	wǎn shang 晚 上
nightclub	*yee-eh zohng - hway*	yè zǒng huì 夜 总 会
nine	*jeo*	jiǔ 九
nineteen	*shir jeo*	shí jiǔ 十 九

ninth	*dee jeo guh*	dì jiǔ gè 第九个
no	*boo*	bù 不
noisy	*tsaow zah*	cáo zá 嘈杂
nonsense	*fay hwah*	fèi huà 废话
nonstop flight	*jir dah hahng - bahn*	zhí dá háng bān 直达航班
noodles	*mee-en tee-aow*	miàn tiáo 面条
noon	*johng woo*	zhōng wǔ 中午
normal	*jung chahng*	zhèng cháng 正常
North America	*Bay may joh*	Běi měi zhōu 北美洲
north	*bay boo duh*	běi bù de 北部的
northern	*bay boo*	běi bù 北部
Norway	*Nwuh way*	Nuó wēi 挪威
nose	*bee zih*	bí zi 鼻子
not enough	*boo goh*	bú gòu 不够
not	*boo*	bù 不
notebook	*bee jee ben*	bǐ jì běn 笔记本

November	*Shir ee yweh*	shí yī yuè 十 一 月
number	*shoo zih*	shù zì 数 字
room number	*fahng jee-en -* *haow mah*	fáng jiān hào mǎ 房 间 号 码
nurse	*hoo shir*	hù shi 护 士
nursery	*twuh ar swuh*	tuō ér suǒ 托 儿 所
nutrition	*ying yahng*	yíng yǎng 营 养
o'clock	*dee-en johng*	diǎn zhōng 点 钟
oatmeal	*mye pee-en*	mài piàn 麦 片
occupation	*jir yee-eh*	zhí yè 职 业
occupied	*jahn jiew*	zhān jù 占 据
ocean	*dah hye*	dà hǎi 大 海
October	*Shir yweh*	shí yuè 十 月
offer (verb)	*tee gohng*	tí gōng 提 供
office hours	*shahng bahn -* *shir jee-en*	shàng bān 上 班 shí jiān 时 间
office worker	*shahng bahn -* *zoo*	shàng bān zú 上 班 族

office	*bahn gohng shir*	bàn gōng shì 办 公 室
officer	*gwahn ywahn*	guān yuán 官 员
official	*gwahn fahng-duh*	guān fāng de 官 方 的
official (people)	*gohng woo -ywahn*	gōng wù yuán 公 务 员
official business	*gwuh yoh -chee yee-eh*	guó yǒu qǐ yè 国 有 企 业
often	*jing chahng*	jīng cháng 经 常
oil	*yoh*	yóu 油
ointment	*yaow gaow*	yào gāo 药 膏
okay	*haow duh*	hǎo de 好 的
old (person)	*laow*	lǎo 老
old (thing)	*jeo*	jiù 旧
old people	*laow ren*	lǎo rén 老 人
on, on top of___	*zye___shahng -mee-en*	zài shàng mian 在 ___ 上 面
once	*ee tsih*	yí cì 一 次
one	*ee*	yī 一

one-child policy	*ee har -*	yī hái ér 一 孩 儿
	jung tsuh	zhèng cè 政 策
one-way ticket	*dahn chung - pee-aow*	dān chéng piào 单 程 票
one-way	*dahn shing - shee-en*	dān xíng xiàn 单 行 线
only	*jir boo gwuh*	zhǐ bú guò 只 不 过
open (business hours)	*kye men*	kāi mén 开 门
open (verb)	*dah kye*	dǎ kāi 打 开
opera	*guh jiew*	gē jù 歌 剧
operation	*shoh shoo*	shǒu shù 手 术
opium	*yah pee-en*	yā piàn 鸦 片
opportunity	*jee hway*	jī huì 机 会
opposite	*shee-ahng - fahn duh*	xiāng fǎn de 相 反 的
orange (color)	*jiew hwahng suh*	jú huáng sè 桔 黄 色
orange (fruit)	*jiew zih*	jú zi 桔 子
orange juice	*jiew zih jir*	jú zi zhī 桔 子 汁
order (a meal)	*dee-en*	diǎn 点

order (directive)	*ming ling*	mìng lìng 命 令
ordinary	*ping chahng - duh*	píng cháng de 平 常 的
organization	*zoo jir*	zǔ zhī 组 织
orgasm	*gaow chaow*	gāo cháo 高 潮
oriental	*dohng fahng - duh*	dōng fāng de 东 方 的
Ottawa	*Wuh tye hwah*	Wò tài huá 渥 太 华
our	*wuh men duh*	wǒ men de 我 们 的
outlet (electric)	*chah zwuh*	chā zuò 插 座
outside	*wye mee-en*	wài miàn 外 面
over___ (preposition)	*zye___shahng - mee-en*	zài shàng mian 在 ___ 上 面
over (done)	*jee-eh shoo*	jié shù 结 束
overcoat	*dah ee*	dà yī 大 衣
overcome	*kuh foo*	kè fú 克 服
overnight	*tohng shee-aow*	tōng xiāo 通 宵
overseas Chinese	*hwah chee-aow*	huá qiáo 华 侨
overseas	*hye wye*	hǎi wài 海 外

owe	*chee-en*	qiàn 欠
owner	*yee-eh joo*	yè zhǔ 业 主
ox	*gohng neo*	gōng niú 公 牛
oxygen	*yahng chee*	yǎng qì 氧 气
oyster	*moo lee*	mǔ lì 牡 蛎
Pacific Ocean	*Tye ping yahng*	Tài píng yáng 太 平 洋
package	*baow gwuh*	bāo guǒ 包 裹
packed	*sye mahn luh*	sāi mǎn le 塞 满 了
pagoda	*tah*	tǎ 塔
pain	*tung tohng*	téng tòng 疼 痛
painful	*hen tohng duh*	hěn tòng de 很 痛 的
paint, draw	*hwah hwah*	huà huà 画 画
painting(noun)	*hwah*	huà 画

pair (translation varies depending on items)

a pair of chopsticks	*ee shwahng -*	yì shuāng 一 双
	kwye zih	kuài zi 筷 子

a pair of jeans	*ee tee-aow -*	yì tiáo 一条
	neo zye koo	niú zǎi kù 牛仔裤
a pair of shoes	*ee shwahng -* *shee-eh*	yì shuāng xié 一双 鞋
pajamas	*shway ee*	shui yī 睡 衣
Pakistan	*Bah jee sih tahn*	Bā jī sī tǎn 巴基斯坦
palace	*gohng dee-en*	gōng diàn 宫 殿
panda bear	*shee-ohng -* *maow*	xióng māo 熊 猫
pants, slacks	*koo zih*	kù zǐ 裤 子
pantyhose	*lee-en koo wah*	lián kù wà 连 裤 袜
papaya	*moo gwah*	mù guā 木 瓜
paper currency	*jir bee*	zhǐ bì 纸 币
paper	*jir*	zhǐ 纸
paradise	*tee-en tahng*	tiān táng 天 堂
parents	*foo moo*	fù mǔ 父 母
Paris	*Bah lee*	Bā lí 巴 黎
park (verb)	*ting chuh*	tíng chē 停 车

park (noun)	*gohng ywahn*	gōng yuán 公 园
parking lot	*ting chuh - chahng*	tíng chē chǎng 停 车 场
partial payment	*fen pee - foo kwahn*	fēn pī fù kuǎn 分 批 付 款
partner	*huh hwuh ren*	hé huǒ rén 合 伙 人
party	*jiew hway*	jù huì 聚 会
passenger	*liew kuh*	lǚ kè 旅 客
passport number	*hoo jaow - haow mah*	hù zhào hào mǎ 护 照 号 码
passport	*hoo jaow*	hù zhào 护 照
past	*gwuh chiew*	guò qù 过 去
pastry shop	*mee-en baow - dee-en*	miàn bāo diàn 面 包 店
patent	*jwahn lee*	zhuān lì 专 利
path	*tohng daow*	tōng dào 通 道
patience	*nye sheen*	nài xīn 耐 心
patient (adjective)	*nye sheen duh*	nài xīn de 耐 心 的
patient (noun)	*bing ren*	bìng rén 病 人
pay (verb)	*foo*	fù 付

payment	*gohng zih*	gōng zī 工 资
pea	*wahn doh*	wān dòu 豌 豆
peace	*huh ping*	hé píng 和 平
peaches	*taow zih*	táo zi 桃 子
peak, summit	*shahn ding*	shān dǐng 山 顶
peanuts	*hwah shung*	huā shēng 花 生
pear	*lee*	lí 梨
Pearl River	*Joo jee-ahng*	Zhū jiāng 珠 江
pearl	*jen joo*	zhēn zhū 珍 珠
peasant	*nohng meen*	nóng mín 农 民
pedestrian	*shing ren*	xíng rén 行 人
Peking duck	*Bay jing - kaow yah*	Běi jīng kǎo yā 北 京 烤 鸭
pen	*gahng bee*	gāng bǐ 钢 笔
pencil	*chee-en bee*	qiān bǐ 铅 笔
penicillin	*ching may soo*	qīng méi sù 青 霉 素
penis	*yeen jing*	yīn jīng 阴 茎

people	*ren men*	rén men 人 们
pepper	*hoo jee-aow fen*	hú jiāo fěn 胡 椒 粉
perfect	*wahn may duh*	wán měi de 完 美 的
performance	*bee-aow yahn*	biǎo yǎn 表 演
performer	*bee-aow yahn - juh*	biǎo yǎn zhě 表 演 者
perfume	*shee-ahng - shway*	xiāng shuǐ 香 水
permission	*shiew kuh*	xǔ kě 许 可
permit (certificate)	*shiew kuh jung*	xǔ kě zhèng 许 可 证
permit (verb)	*ywin shiew*	yǔn xǔ 允 许
personal	*sih ren duh*	sī rén de 私 人 的
personality	*guh shing*	gè xìng 个 性
personally	*cheen zih duh*	qīn zì de 亲 自 的
petroleum	*shir yoh*	shí yóu 石 油
pharmacy	*yaow dee-en*	yào diàn 药 店
Philadelphia	*Fay chung*	Fèi chéng 费 城
Philippines	*Fay liew been*	Fēi lù bīn 菲 律 宾

phone (noun)	*dee-en hwah*	diàn huà 电 话
phone (verb)	*dah - dee-en hwah*	dǎ diàn huà 打 电 话
phone call (long-distance)	*chahng too - dee-en hwah*	cháng tú 长 途 diàn huà 电 话
phone card (long-distance)	*chahng too - dee-en hwah - kah*	cháng tú 长 途 diàn huà kǎ 电 话 卡
photo	*jaow pee-en*	zhào piàn 照 片
photocopy	*foo yeen*	fù yìn 复 印
physical exam	*tee jee-en*	tǐ jiǎn 体 检
physical exercise	*dwahn lee-en - shen tee*	duàn liàn shēn tǐ 锻 炼 身 体
picnic	*yee-eh tsahn*	yě cān 野 餐
picture	*hwah*	huà 画
picture (photo)	*jaow pee-en*	zhào piàn 照 片
piece	*kwye* or *jahng*	kuài zhāng 块 ; 张
pig	*joo*	zhū 猪
pigeon	*guh zih*	gē zi 鸽 子

pill	*yaow peer*	yào piàn er 药 片 儿
pillow	*jen toh*	zhěn tou 枕 头
pillowcase	*jen taow*	zhěn tào 枕 套
pineapple	*boo lwuh*	bō luó 菠 萝
ping-pong	*ping pahng - cheo*	pīng pāng qiú 乒 乓 球
place	*dee fahng*	dì fang 地 方
plane	*fay jee*	fēi jī 飞 机
plants	*jir woo*	zhí wù 植 物
plastic bag	*soo lee-aow dye*	sù liào dài 塑 料 袋
plate	*pahn zih*	pán zi 盘 子
platform (train)	*jahn tye*	zhàn tái 站 台
play (verb)	*wahn*	wán 玩
player, athlete	*ywin dohng - ywahn*	yùn dòng yuán 运 动 员
playground	*tsaow chahng*	cāo chǎng 操 场
please	*ching*	qǐng 请
plug	*chah toh*	chā tóu 插 头

plum	*lee zih*	lǐ zi 李 子
pneumonia	*fay yahn*	fèi yán 肺 炎
poached egg	*huh baow dahn*	hé bāo dàn 荷 包 蛋
pocket	*doh*	dōu 兜
poems, songs	*shir guh*	shī gē 诗 歌
poet	*shir ren*	shī rén 诗 人
point (noun)	*dee-en*	diǎn 点
poison (noun)	*doo*	dú 毒
Poland	*Bwuh lahn*	Bō lán 波 兰
police station	*jing chah jiew*	jǐng chá jú 警 察 局
police	*jing chah*	jǐng chá 警 察
politician	*jung kuh*	zhèng kè 政 客
politics	*jung jir*	zhèng zhì 政 治
pollution	*woo rahn*	wū rǎn 污 染
pool (swimming)	*yoh yohng chir*	yóu yǒng chí 游 泳 池
poor	*chee-ohng*	qióng 穷

population	*ren koh*	rén kǒu 人 口	
porcelain	*tsih chee*	cí qì 瓷 器	
pork	*joo roh*	zhū ròu 猪 肉	
port	*gahng koh*	gǎng kǒu 港 口	
Portugal	*Poo taow yah*	Pú táo yá 葡 萄 牙	
post office	*yoh jiew*	yóu jú 邮 局	
postage stamp	*yoh pee-aow*	yóu piào 邮 票	
postage	*yoh zih*	yóu zī 邮 资	
postcard	*ming sheen - pee-en*	míng xìn piàn 明 信 片	
potato	*too doh*	tǔ dòu 土 豆	
pottery	*taow chee*	táo qì 陶 器	
pound (British currency)	*ying bahng*	yīng bàng 英 磅	
prawn	*dway shee-ah*	duì xiā 对 虾	
practise	*lee-en shee*	liàn xí 练 习	
predicate	*yiew tsuh*	yù cè 预 测	
pregnant	*hwye ywin*	huái yùn 怀 孕	

premier (national)	*zohng lee*	zǒng lǐ 总 理
prepare	*jwun bay*	zhǔn bèi 准 备
prescription	*yaow fahng*	yào fāng 药 方
present (gift)	*lee woo*	lǐ wù 礼 物
present (verb)	*chung shee-en*	chéng xiàn 呈 现
present (time)	*shee-en zye - duh*	xiàn zài de 现 在 的
president (corporate)	*zohng tsye*	zǒng cái 总 裁
president (national)	*zohng tohng*	zǒng tǒng 总 统
pressure	*yah lee*	yā lì 压 力
pretty	*pee-aow - lee-ahng*	piào liang 漂 亮
price	*jee-ah guh*	jià gé 价 格
priest	*moo shir*	mù shī 牧 师
primary school	*shee-aow shweh*	xiǎo xué 小 学
print	*dah yeen*	dǎ yìn 打 印
prison	*jee-en yiew*	jiān yù 监 狱
private	*sih ren duh*	sī rén de 私 人 的

problems	**wen tee**	wèn tí 问 题
process (noun)	**gwuh chung**	guò chéng 过 程
product	**chahn peen**	chǎn pǐn 产 品
profession	**jir yee-eh**	zhí yè 职 业
professional	**jwahn yee-eh - duh**	zhuān yè de 专 业 的
profit	**lee rwun**	lì rùn 利 润
program	**chung shiew**	chéng xù 程 序
promise	**dah ying**	dā ying 答 应
promises	**chung nwuh**	chéng nuò 承 诺
pronouns	**dye tsih**	dài cí 代 词
pronunciation	**fah yeen**	fā yīn 发 音
property	**tsye chahn**	cái chǎn 财 产
prostitute	**jee niew**	jì nǚ 妓 女
provide	**gohng ying**	gòng yìng 供 应
province	**shung**	shěng 省
psychology	**sheen lee shweh**	xīn lǐ xué 心 理 学

public relations	*gohng gohng - gwahn shee*	gōng gòng 公 共 guān xì 关 系
Public Security Bureau	*Ahn chwahn - Jiew*	An quán jú 安 全 局
public square	*gwahng chahng*	guǎng chǎng 广 场
public	*gohng johng*	gōng zhòng 公 众
publish	*choo bahn*	chū bǎn 出 版
purchase	*mye*	mǎi 买
purse, handbag	*shoh tee baow*	shǒu tí bāo 手 提 包
quality	*jlr lee-ahng*	zhì liàng 质 量
quantity	*shoo lee-ahng*	shù liàng 数 量
quarter	*sih fen jir ee*	sì fēn zhī yī 四 分 之 一
question (noun)	*wen tee*	wèn tí 问 题
quick	*kwye*	kuài 快
quiet	*ahn jing duh*	ān jìng de 安 静 的
quilt	*mee-en bay*	mián bèi 棉 被
quit (a job)	*tsih jir*	cí zhí 辞 职

quiz, test	*tsuh yahn*	cè yàn 测 验
quota	*pay uh*	pèi é 配 额
race (match)	*bee sye*	bǐ sài 比 赛
race (nationality)	*johng zoo*	zhòng zú 种 族
racist	*johng zoo -* *joo ee juh*	zhòng zú 种 族 zhǔ yì zhě 主 义 者
radio	*shoh yeen jee*	shōu yīn jī 收 音 机
railway station	*hwuh chuh jahn*	huǒ chē zhàn 火 车 站
railway	*tee-eh loo*	tiě lù 铁 路
rain (noun)	*yiew*	yǔ 雨
raining	*shee-ah yiew*	xià yǔ 下 雨
rainbow	*tsye hohng*	cǎi hóng 彩 虹
raincoat	*yiew ee*	yǔ yī 雨 衣
rainstorm	*baow fung yiew*	bào fēng yǔ 暴 风 雨
raisin	*poo taow gahn*	pú tao gān 葡 萄 干
rape	*chee-ahng jee-en*	qiáng jiān 强 奸

rash	*tsohng mahng - duh*	cōng máng de 匆 忙 的
rat	*laow shoo*	lǎo shǔ 老 鼠
rate	*jee-ah guh*	jià gé 价 格
raw	*shung duh*	shēng de 生 的
razor blades	*daow pee-en*	dāo piàn 刀 片
razor	*tee shiew daow*	tì xū dāo 剃 须 刀
read	*doo* or *kahn*	dú kàn 读 ; 看
reader	*doo juh*	dú zhě 读 者
ready	*jwun bay haow - luh*	zhǔn bèi hǎo le 准 备 好 了
real	*jen duh*	zhēn de 真 的
really	*jen duh*	zhēn de 真 地
realtor	*fahng dee chahn - jing jee ren*	fáng dì chǎn 房 地 产 jīng jì rén 经 纪 人
receipt	*fah pee-aow*	fā piào 发 票
receptionist	*jee-eh dye - ywahn*	jiē dài yuán 接 待 员
recommend	*tway jee-en*	tuī jiàn 推 荐

record (noun)	*jee loo*	jì lù 纪 录
to record audio	*loo yeen*	lù yīn 录 音
to record video	*loo shee-ahng*	lù xiàng 录 像
recreation	*shee-aow - chee-en*	xiāo qiǎn 消 遣
refrigerator	*bing shee-ahng*	bīng xiāng 冰 箱
refugee	*nahn meen*	nàn mín 难 民
refund	*gway hwahn*	guī huán 归 还
region	*dee chiew*	dì qū 地 区
registered mail	*gwah haow - sheen*	guà hào xìn 挂 号 信
regulation	*gway zuh*	guī zé 规 则
relationship	*gwahn shee*	guān xì 关 系
relative (kin)	*cheen chee*	qīn qi 亲 戚
relax	*fahng sohng*	fàng sōng 放 松
religion	*zohng jee-aow*	zōng jiào 宗 教
remember	*jee joo*	jì zhù 记 住
rent money	*zoo jeen*	zū jīn 租 金

rent (verb)	*zoo*	zū 租
repair	*sheo lee*	xiū lǐ 修 理
repeat	*chohng foo*	chóng fù 重 复
representative	*dye bee-aow*	dài biǎo 代 表
reservation	*yiew ding*	yù dìng 预 定
reserve	*yiew ding*	yù dìng 预 定
residence permit	*jiew leo jung*	jū liú zhèng 居 留 证
green card	*liew kah*	lǜ kǎ 绿 卡
residential area	*joo jye chiew*	zhù zhái qū 住 宅 区
resource	*zih ywahn*	zī yuán 资 源
responsibility	*zuh ren*	zé rèn 责 任
rest	*sheo shee*	xiū xī 休 息
restaurant	*tsahn gwahn*	cān guǎn 餐 馆
return ticket	*wahng fahn - pee-aow*	wǎng fǎn piào 往 返 票
return	*hway lye*	huí lái 回 来
return (give back)	*hwahn*	hái 还

reverse charges	*dway fahng - foo kwahn*	duì fāng fù kuǎn 对 方 付 款
revolution	*guh ming*	gé mìng 革 命
rice (cooked)	*mee fahn*	mǐ fàn 米 饭
rice (uncooked)	*dah mee*	dà mǐ 大 米
rich	*yoh chee-en*	yǒu qián 有 钱
ride	*chee*	qí 骑
right (correct)	*dway*	duì 对
right (direction)	*yoh*	yòu 右
rights (human rights)	*chwahn lee*	quán lì 权 利
ring (jewelry)	*jee-eh jir*	jiè zhi 戒 指
river	*huh*	hé 河
road	*loo*	lù 路
roast; roasted	*kaow*	kǎo 烤
rob	*chee-ahng*	qiǎng 抢
rock and roll	*yaow gwun*	yáo gǔn 摇 滚
roof	*fahng ding*	fáng dǐng 房 顶

room number	***fahng jee-en - haow***	fáng jiān hào 房 间 号
room	***fahng jee-en***	fáng jiān 房 间
roommate	***tohng woo***	tóng wū 同 屋
rose	***may gway***	méi guī 玫 瑰
rotten	***foo lahn***	fù làn 腐 烂
round-trip	***wahng fahn - liew shing***	wǎng fǎn lǚ xíng 往 返 旅 行
route	***loo shee-en***	lù xiàn 路 线
rubbish	***lah jee***	lā jī 垃 圾
rude	***yee-eh mahn duh***	yě mán de 野 蛮 的
rug	***dee-en zih***	diàn zi 垫 子
ruins	***fay shiew***	fèi xū 废 墟
rule	***gway zuh***	guī zé 规 则
run	***paow***	pǎo 跑
sack, bag	***dye zih***	dài zi 袋 子
safe (adj.)	***ahn chwahn duh***	ān quán de 安 全 的
safe (noun)	***baow shee-en - shee-ahng***	bǎo xiǎn xiāng 保 险 箱

safety	*ahn chwahn*	ǎn quán 安 全
salad	*shah lah*	shā lā 沙 拉
salary	*gohng zih*	gōng zī 工 资
sale	*shee-aow shoh*	xiāo shòu 销 售
sales manager	*shee-aow shoh - jing lee*	xiāo shòu jīng lǐ 销 售 经 理
sales tax	*ying yee-eh - shway*	yíng yè shuì 营 业 税
salesperson	*shoh hwuh - ywahn*	shòu huò yuán 售 货 员
salmon	*sahn wen yiew*	sān wén yú 三 文 鱼
salt	*yahn*	yán 盐
same	*ee yahng*	yí yàng 一 样
sample	*yahng peen*	yàng pǐn 样 品
San Francisco	*Jeo jeen shahn*	Jiù jīn shān 旧 金 山
sandals	*lee-ahng - shee-eh*	liáng xié 凉 鞋
sandwich	*sahn ming jir*	sān míng zhì 三 明 治
sanitary towel	*way shung jeen*	wèi shēng jīn 卫 生 巾
satellite	*ren zaow - way shing*	rén zào wèi xīng 人 造 卫 星

Saturday	*Shing chee leo*	xīng qī liù 星 期 六
sausage	*shee-ahng - chahng*	xiāng cháng 香 肠
save money	*shung chee-en*	shěng qián 省 钱
save, rescue	*jeo*	jiù 救
say	*shwuh*	shuō 说
scar	*shahng bah*	shāng bā 伤 疤
scenery	*fung jing*	fēng jǐng 风 景
schedule	*shir jee-en - bee-aow*	shí jiān biǎo 时 间 表
scholar	*shweh juh*	xué zhě 学 者
scholarship	*jee-ahng shweh - jeen*	jiǎng xué jīn 奖 学 金
school	*shweh shee-aow*	xué xiào 学 校
schoolmate	*shee-aow yoh*	xiào yǒu 校 友
scientist	*kuh shweh - jee-ah*	kē xué jiā 科学家
scissors	*jee-en daow*	jiǎn dāo 剪 刀
scrambled eggs	*chaow jee dahn*	chǎo jī dàn 炒 鸡 蛋
screwdriver	*lwuh sih daow*	luó sī dāo 螺 丝 刀

sculpture	*dee-aow soo*	diāo sù 雕 塑
sea	*dah hye*	dà hǎi 大 海
seafood	*hye shee-en*	hǎi xiān 海 鲜
seashore, beach	*hye tahn*	hǎi tān 海 滩
seasick	*ywin chwahn*	yūn chuán 晕 船
season	*jee jee-eh*	jì jié 季 节
seat	*zwuh way*	zuò wèi 座 位
seatbelt	*ahn chwahn dye*	ān quán dài 安 全 带
second (placement)	*dee ar*	dì èr 第 二
second (measurement of time)	*mee-aow*	miǎo 秒
secret	*mee mee*	mì mì 秘 密
secretary	*mee shoo*	mì shū 秘 书
section, part	*boo fen*	bù fen 部 分
security guard	*baow ahn*	bǎo ān 保 安
see	*kahn jee-en*	kàn jiàn 看 见
sell	*mye*	mài 卖

send (post)	*jee*	jì 寄
send back	*tway hwahn*	tuì hái 退 还
send C.O.D.	*hwuh daow - foo kwahn*	huò dào fù kuǎn 货 到 付 款
sentence (noun)	*jiew zih*	jù zi 句 子
sentence (verb)	*pahn jweh*	pàn jué 判 决
Seoul	*Hahn chung* or *Shoh ar*	Hàn chéng 汉 城 ; shǒu ěr 首 尔
separate (verb)	*fen kye*	fēn kāi 分 开
September	*Jeo yweh*	jiǔ yuè 九 月
serious	*yahn soo duh*	yán sù de 严 肃 的
service attendant	*foo woo ywahn*	fú wù yuán 服 务 员
service fee	*foo woo fay*	fú wù fèi 服 务 费
service	*foo woo*	fú wù 服 务
seven	*chee*	qī 七
seventeen	*shir chee*	shí qī 十 七
seventh	*dee chee guh*	dì qī gè 第 七 个

253

several	*jee guh*	jǐ gè 几 个
sew	*fung*	féng 缝
sex	*shing*	xìng 性
sexy	*shing gahn*	xìng gǎn 性 感
shake hands	*wuh shoh*	wò shǒu 握 手
shampoo	*shee fah - shee-ahng bwuh*	xǐ fà xiāng bō 洗 发 香 波
Shanghai	*Shahng hye*	Shàng hǎi 上 海
share	*fen shee-ahng*	fēn xiǎng 分 享
shark's fin	*yiew chir*	yú chì 鱼 翅
shave	*gwah lee-en*	guā liǎn 刮 脸
she	*tah*	tā 她
sheep	*mee-en yahng*	mián yáng 绵 羊
sheet	*chwahng dahn*	chuáng dān 床 单
Shenzhen	*Shen jen*	Shēn zhèn 深 圳
ship	*lwun chwahn*	lún chuán 轮 船
shipment	*jwahng chwahn*	zhuāng chuán 装 船

shirt	*chen ee*	chèn yī 衬衣
shit	*shir*	shǐ 屎
Shit!	*Tah mah duh!*	Tā mā de 他妈的!
shoelaces	*shee-eh dar*	xié dài er 鞋带儿
shoes	*shee-eh*	xié 鞋
shop (noun)	*shahng dee-en*	shāng diàn 商店
shopping area	*shahng yee-eh -chiew*	shāng yè qū 商业区
shopping	*mye dohng shee*	mǎi dōng xi 买东西
short (height)	*eye*	ǎi 矮
short (distance)	*dwahn*	duǎn 短
shorts	*dwahn koo*	duǎn kù 短裤
show___ (verb)	*gay___kahn -kahn*	gěi ___ kàn kan 给 ___ 看看
shower	*leen yiew*	lín yù 淋浴
shrimp	*shee-ah*	xiā 虾
Shut up!	*Bee zway!*	Bì zuǐ 闭嘴!
shut	*gwahn shahng*	guān shàng 关上

shy	*hye sheo*	hài xiū 害 羞
Siberia	*Shee bwuh - lee yah*	Xī bó lì yà 西 伯 利 亚
sick (mentally)	*bee-en tye*	biàn tài 变 态
sick (physically)	*bing luh*	bìng le 病 了
sidewalk	*ren shing daow*	rén xíng dào 人 行 道
sightseeing	*gwahn gwahng*	guān guāng 观 光
sign (noun)	*bee-aow jee*	biāo jì 标 记
sign (verb)	*chee-ahn zih*	qiān zì 签 字
signature	*chee-en ming*	qiān míng 签 名
silent	*chen mwuh*	chén mò 沉 默
silk factory	*sih choh chahng*	sī chóu chǎng 丝 绸 厂
Silk Road	*Sih choh Jir loo*	Sī chóu zhī lù 丝 绸 之 路
silk	*sih choh*	sī chóu 丝 绸
silver	*yeen zih*	yín zi 银 子
simple	*jee-en dahn duh*	jiǎn dān de 简 单 的
sing	*chahng guh*	chàng gē 唱 歌

Singapore	*Sheen jee-ah - pwuh*	Xīn jiā pō 新加坡
single room	*dahn ren - fahng jee-en*	dān rén fáng jiān 单人房间
single ticket	*dahn chung - pee-aow*	dān chéng piào 单程票
single, unmarried	*dahn shen*	dān shēn 单身
sister (older)	*jee-eh jee-eh*	jiě jie 姐姐
sister (younger)	*may may*	mèi mei 妹妹
sit	*zwuh*	zuò 坐
situation	*ching kwahng*	qíng kuàng 情况
six	*leo*	liù 六
sixteen	*shir leo*	shí liù 十六
sixth	*dee leo guh*	dì liù gè 第六个
size	*dah shee-aow*	dà xiǎo 大小
skating	*leo bing*	liū bīng 溜冰
ski (snow)	*hwah shweh*	huá xuě 滑雪
ski (water)	*hwah shway*	huá shuǐ 滑水
skin	*pee foo*	pí fū 皮肤

skirt	*chwin zih*	qún zi 裙 子
sky	*tee-en kohng*	tiān kōng 天 空
slang	*lee yiew*	lǐ yǔ 俚 语
sleep	*shway jee-aow*	shuì jiào 睡 觉
sleeper	*wuh poo*	wò pù 卧 铺
sleeping car (train)	*wuh poo chuh - shee-ahng*	wò pù chē xiāng 卧 铺 车 厢
sleepy	*kwun*	kùn 困
sleeves	*sheo zih*	xiù zi 袖 子
slipper	*twuh shee-eh*	tuō xié 拖 鞋
slogan	*bee-aow yiew*	biāo yǔ 标 语
slow	*mahn*	màn 慢
small change	*ling chee-en*	líng qián 零 钱
small	*shee-aow*	xiǎo 小
smaller	*gung shee-aow - duh*	gèng xiǎo de 更 小 的
smell (noun)	*way daow*	wèi dào 味 道
smell (verb)	*wen*	wén 闻

smelly	*choh*	chòu 臭
smile	*way shee-aow*	wēi xiào 微 笑
smoke (noun)	*yahn*	yān 烟
smoking	*choh yahn*	chōu yān 抽 烟
snack	*shee-aow chir*	xiǎo chī 小 吃
snake	*shuh*	shé 蛇
snow	*shweh*	xuě 雪
snowing	*shee-ah shweh*	xià xuě 下 雪
so	*swuh ee*	suǒ yǐ 所 以
soap	*shee-ahng zaow*	xiāng zào 香 皂
soccer	*zoo cheo*	zú qiú 足 球
socialism	*shuh hway - joo ee*	shè huì zhǔ yì 社 会 主 义
socket (electric)	*chah zwuh*	chā zuò 插 座
socks	*wah zih*	wà zi 袜 子
soda water	*chee shway*	qì shuǐ 汽 水
sofa	*shah fah*	shā fā 沙 发

soft	*rwahn*	ruǎn 软
soft drink	*rwahn - yeen lee-aow*	ruǎn yǐn liào 软 饮 料
software	*rwahn jee-en*	ruǎn jiàn 软 件
soldier	*jwin ren*	jūn rén 军 人
some	*ee shee-eh*	yì xiē 一 些
something	*shir ching*	shì qíng 事 情
son	*ar zih*	ér zi 儿 子
song lyrics	*guh tsih*	gē cí 歌 词
song	*guh*	gē 歌
son-in-law	*niew shiew*	nǚ xù 女 婿
soon	*hen kwye*	hěn kuài 很 快
sore	*tung*	téng 疼
sorry (apology)	*baow chee-en*	bào qiàn 报 歉
sorry (regret)	*ee hahn*	yí hàn 遗 憾
sound	*shung yeen*	shēng yīn 声 音
soup	*tahng*	tāng 汤

sour	*swahn*	suān 酸
South Africa	*Nahn fay*	Nán fēi 南 非
south	*nahn boo duh*	nán bù de 南 部 的
souvenir shop	*jee nee-en peen -*	jì niàn pǐn 纪 念 品
	shahng dee-en	shāng diàn 商 店
souvenir	*jee nee-en peen*	jì niàn pǐn 纪 念 品
soy sauce	*jee-ahng yoh*	jiàng yóu 酱 油
Spain	*Shee bahn yah*	Xī bān yá 西 班 牙
spare time	*yee-eh yiew -* *shir jee-en*	yè yú shí jiān 业 余 时 间
speak	*shwuh*	shuō 说
speakers (stereo)	*yeen shee-ahng*	yīn xiāng 音 箱
special	*tuh bee-eh duh*	tè bié de 特 别 的
specifically	*ming chweh duh*	míng què de 明 确 的
spicy	*lah*	là 辣
spinach	*bwuh tsye*	bō cài 菠 菜
spit	*too tahn*	tǔ tán 吐 痰

spoon	*shaow zih*	sháo zi 勺 子
sporting goods	*tee yiew - yohng peen*	tǐ yù yòng pǐn 体 育 用 品
sports field	*ywin dohng - chahng*	yùn dòng chǎng 运 动 场
sports	*ywin dohng*	yùn dòng 运 动
sprain	*neo shahng*	niǔ shāng 扭 伤
spring (water)	*chwahn shway*	quán shuī 泉 水
Spring Festival	*Chwun jee-eh*	chūn jié 春 节
spring	*chwun tee-en*	chūn tiān 春 天
square (place)	*gwahng chahng*	guǎng chǎng 广 场
squid	*yoh yiew*	yóu yú 鱿 鱼
stadium	*tee yiew chahng*	tǐ yù chǎng 体 育 场
stairs	*tye jee-eh*	tái jiē 台 阶
stale	*boo sheen - shee-en duh*	bù xīn xiān de 不 新 鲜 的
stamp (noun)	*yoh pee-aow*	yóu piào 邮 票
stand in line	*pye dway*	pái duì 排 队
standard (level or quality)	*bee-aow jwun*	biāo zhǔn 标 准

star	*shing shing*	xīng xing 星 星
Starbucks	*Shing bah kuh*	Xīng bā kè 星 巴 克
stare	*ding juh kahn*	dīng zháo kàn 盯 着 看
start	*kye shir*	kāi shǐ 开 始
station	*chuh jahn*	chē zhàn 车 站
stationary store	*wen jiew dee-en*	wén jù diàn 文 具 店
statue	*dee-aow soo*	diāo sù 雕 塑
stay at / with___	*dye zye___*	dài zài ___ 待 在 ___
steak	*neo pye*	niú pái 牛 排
steal	*toh*	tōu 偷
steamed bun	*mahn toh*	mán tou 馒 头
stereo	*yeen shee-ahng*	yīn xiǎng 音 响
stir-fried	*chaow*	chǎo 炒
stomach	*doo zih*	dù zi 肚 子
stomach ache	*doo zih tung*	dù zi téng 肚 子 疼
stop	*ting*	tíng 停

263

store (shop)	*shahng dee-en*	shāng diàn 商 店	
store (verb)	*choo tsahng*	chǔ cáng 储 藏	
storm	*baow fung yiew*	bào fēng yǔ 暴 风 雨	
story	*goo shir*	gù shì 故 事	
stove	*loo zih*	lú zi 炉 子	
straight ahead	*ee jir*	yì zhí 一 直	
straight forward	*tahn shwye duh*	tǎn shuài de 坦 率 的	
stranger	*mwuh shung ren*	mò shēng rén 陌 生 人	
strawberries	*tsaow may*	cǎo méi 草 莓	
street	*jee-eh daow*	jiē dào 街 道	
strict	*yee-en lee duh*	yán lì de 严 厉 的	
strong	*chee-ahng - jwahng duh*	qiáng zhuàng de 强 壮 的	
student	*shweh shung*	xué shēng 学 生	
study abroad	*leo shweh*	liú xué 留 学	
study	*shweh shee*	xué xí 学 习	
style, appearance	*fung guh*	fēng gé 风 格	

subject	*kuh moo*	kē mù 科目
subtitles	*zih moo*	zì mù 字幕
suburbs	*jee-aow chiew*	jiāo qū 郊区
subway station	*dee tee-eh jahn*	dì tiě zhàn 地铁站
subway	*dee tee-eh*	dì tiě 地铁
success	*chung gohng*	chéng gōng 成功
sugar	*tahng*	táng 糖
suit (western style)	*shee foo*	xī fú 西服
suitcase	*pee shee-ahng*	pí xiāng 皮箱
suite	*taow fahng*	tào fáng 套房
Summer Palace	*Ee huh ywahn*	Yí hé yuán 颐和园
summer	*shee-ah tee-en*	xià tiān 夏天
sun	*tye yahng*	tài yáng 太阳
sunburn	*shye shahng luh*	shài shāng le 晒伤了
Sunday	*shing chee rr* or *shing chee -* *tee-en*	xīng qī rì； 星期日； xīng qī tiān 星期天

sunglasses	*tye yahng jing*	tài yáng jìng 太 阳 镜
sunset	*rr lwuh*	rì luò 日 落
sunshine	*yahng gwahng*	yáng guāng 阳 光
suntan lotion	*fahng shye - shwahng*	fáng shài shuāng 防 晒 霜
supermarket	*chaow shir*	chāo shì 超 市
surface mail	*poo tohng - yoh jee-en*	pǔ tōng yóu jiàn 普 通 邮 件
sweat (noun)	*hahn*	hàn 汗
sweat (verb)	*choo hahn*	chū hàn 出 汗
sweater	*maow ee*	máo yī 毛 衣
Sweden	*Rway dee-en*	Ruì diǎn 瑞 典
sweet	*tee-en*	tián 甜
swim	*yoh yohng*	yóu yǒng 游 泳
swimming pool	*yoh yohng chir*	yóu yǒng chí 游 泳 池
swimsuit	*yoh yohng ee*	yóu yǒng yī 游 泳 衣
switch (noun)	*kye gwahn*	kāi guān 开 关
switch off	*gwahn shahng*	guān shàng 关 上

switch on	*dah kye*	dǎ kāi 打 开
Switzerland	*Rway shir*	Ruì shì 瑞 士
swollen	*johng luh*	zhǒng le 肿 了
Sydney	*Shee nee*	Xī ní 悉 尼
symphony	*jee-aow - shee-ahng yweh*	jiāo xiǎng yuè 交 响 乐
symptoms (illness)	*jung jwahng*	zhèng zhuàng 症 状
system	*shee tohng*	xì tǒng 系 统
syrup	*tahng jee-ahng*	táng jiāng 糖 浆
table lamp	*tye dung*	tái dēng 台 灯
table tennis	*ping pahng cheo*	pīng pāng qiú 乒 乓 球
table	*jwuh zih*	zhuō zi 桌 子
tablecloth	*jwuh boo*	zhuō bù 桌 布
tailor	*tsye fung*	cái feng 裁 缝
take away	*nah zoh*	ná zǒu 拿 走
take	*nah*	ná 拿
tangerine	*jiew zih*	jú zi 橘 子

Taoism	*Daow jee-aow*	dào jiào 道 教
tape recorder	*loo yeen jee*	lù yīn jī 录 音 机
tariff	*gwahn shway*	guān shuì 关 税
taste (flavor)	*way daow*	wèi dào 味 道
taste (style)	*peen way*	pǐn wèi 品 味
taste (verb)	*chahng*	cháng 尝
tax free	*mee-en shway*	miǎn shuì 免 税
tax	*shway*	shuì 税
taxi	*choo zoo chuh*	chū zū chē 出 租 车
tea house	*chah gwahn*	chá guǎn 茶 馆
tea	*chah*	chá 茶
teach	*jee-aow*	jiāo 教
teacher	*laow shir*	lǎo shī 老 师
teacup	*chah bay*	chá bēi 茶 杯
team	*dway*	duì 队
teapot	*chah hoo*	chá hú 茶 壶

technology	*jee shoo*	jì shù 技 术
telephone call (long distance)	*chahng too - dee-en hwah*	cháng tú diàn huà 长 途 电 话
telephone directory	*dee-en hwah - boo*	diàn huà bù 电 话 簿
telephone	*dee-en hwah*	diàn huà 电 话
public phone	*gohng yohng - dee-en hwah*	gōng yòng diàn huà 公 用 电 话
television	*dee-en shir*	diàn shì 电 视
tell	*gaow soo*	gào sù 告 诉
temperature	*wen doo*	wēn dù 温 度
temple	*mee-aow*	miào 庙
ten	*shir*	shí 十
tennis court	*wahng cheo - chahng*	wǎng qiú chǎng 网 球 场
tennis match	*wahng cheo sye*	wǎng qiú sài 网 球 赛
tennis	*wahng cheo*	wǎng qiú 网 球
tenth	*dee shir guh*	dì shí gè 第 十 个
test	*tsuh shir*	cè shì 测 试
tetanus	*pwuh shahng - fung*	pò shāng fēng 破 伤 风

text	**kuh wen**	^{kè} ^{wén} 课 文
Thailand	**Tye gwuh**	^{Tài} ^{guó} 泰 国
Thank you.	**Shee-eh shee-eh nee.**	^{Xiè} ^{xiè} ^{nǐ} 谢 谢 你 。
thank	**shee-eh shee-eh**	^{xiè} ^{xiè} 谢 谢
that	**nah guh**	^{nà} ^{gè} 那 个
theater ticket	**shee pee-aow**	^{xì} ^{piào} 戏 票
theater	**shee ywahn**	^{xì} ^{yuàn} 戏 院
their	**tah men duh**	^{tā} ^{men de} 他 们 的
them	**tah men**	^{tā} ^{men} 他 们
there is, are	**yoh**	^{yǒu} 有
there	**nah lee**	^{nà} ^{lǐ} 那 里
thermometer	**wen doo jee**	^{wēn} ^{dù} ^{jì} 温 度 计
thermos bottle	**nwahn shway - ping**	^{nuǎn} ^{shuǐ} ^{píng} 暖 水 瓶
these	**nah shee-eh**	^{nà} ^{xiē} 那 些
they	**tah men**	^{tā} ^{men} 他 们
thick	**hoh**	^{hòu} 厚

thief	*shee-aow toh*	xiǎo tōu 小 偷
thin (not fat)	*shoh*	shòu 瘦
thin (not thick)	*baow*	báo 薄
things	*dohng shee*	dōng xi 东 西
think	*shee-ahng*	xiǎng 想
third	*dee sahn guh*	dì sān gè 第 三 个
thirsty	*kuh*	kě 渴
thirteen	*shir sahn*	shí sān 十 三
this	*juh guh*	zhè ge 这 个
those	*nah shee-eh*	nà xiē 那 些
thousand	*chee-en*	qiān 千
thousand-year egg	*sohng hwah dahn*	sōng huā dàn 松 花 蛋
thread	*shee-en*	xiàn 线
three	*sahn*	sān 三
throat	*sahng zih*	sǎng zi 嗓 子
thumb	*dah moo jir*	dà mǔ zhǐ 大 拇 指

thumbtack	*too ding*	tú dīng 图 钉
thunder	*lay*	léi 雷
thunderstorm	*lay yiew*	léi yǔ 雷 雨
Thursday	*Shing chee sih*	xīng qī sì 星 期 四
Tiananmen	*Tee-en ahn men*	Tiān ān mén 天 安 门
Tianjin	*Tee-en jeen*	Tiān jīn 天 津
Tibet	*Shee zahng*	Xī zàng 西 藏
ticket	*pee-aow*	piào 票
ticket agency	*jee pee-aow - dye lee*	jī piào dài lǐ 机 票 代 理
ticket office	*shoh pee-aow - choo*	shòu piào chù 售 票 处
tide	*chaow shway*	cháo shuǐ 潮 水
tie (noun)	*ling dye*	lǐng dài 领 带
tie (verb)	*jee*	jì 系
tiger	*laow hoo*	lǎo hǔ 老 虎
time	*shir jee-en*	shí jiān 时 间
timetable	*shir jee-en - bee-aow*	shí jiān biǎo 时 间 表

English	Pronunciation	Pinyin	Chinese
tin, can	gwahn toh	guàn tou	罐 头
tip (gratuity)	shee-aow fay	xiǎo fèi	小 费
tired	lay luh	lèi le	累 了
tissue paper	tsahn jeen jir	cān jīn zhǐ	餐 巾 纸
toast (toasted bread)	kaow mee-en - baow peer	kǎo miàn bāo piàn	烤 面 包 片
today	jeen tee-en	jīn tiān	今 天
toe	jee-aow jir	jiǎo zhǐ	脚 趾
together	ee chee	yì qǐ	一 起
toilet	tsuh swuh	cè suǒ	厕 所
toilet paper	way shung jir	wèi shēng zhǐ	卫 生 纸
Tokyo	Dohng jing	Dōng jīng	东 京
tomato	shee hohng shir	xī hóng shì	西 红 柿
tomato juice	shee hohng - shir jir	xī hóng shì zhī	西 红 柿 汁
tomb	fen moo	fén mù	坟 墓
tomorrow	ming tee-en	míng tiān	明 天
tongue	shuh toh	shé tou	舌 头

SPEAK E-Z CHINESE

tonight	*jeen wahn*	jīn wǎn 今 晚
too (amount)	*tye*	tài 太
too (also)	*yee-eh*	yě 也
tool	*gohng jiew*	gōng jù 工 具
tooth	*yah chir*	yá chǐ 牙 齿
toothache	*yah tung*	yá téng 牙 疼
toothbrush	*yah shwah*	yá shuā 牙 刷
toothpaste	*yah gaow*	yá gāo 牙 膏
toothpick	*yah chee-en*	yá qiān 牙 签
torch, flashlight	*shoh dee-en*	shǒu diàn 手 电
Toronto	*Dwuh lwun - dwuh*	Duō lún duō 多 伦 多
total	*zohng jee*	zǒng jì 总 计
tour escort	*ling dway*	lǐng duì 领 队
tour	*liew shing*	lǚ xíng 旅 行
tourist	*yoh kuh*	you kè 游 客
tournament	*lee-en sye*	lián sài 联 赛

towel	*maow jeen*	máo jīn 毛 巾
tower	*tah*	tǎ 塔
town	*chung jen*	chéng zhèn 城 镇
toy store	*wahn jiew - dee-en*	wán jù diàn 玩 具 店
toy	*wahn jiew*	wán jù 玩 具
track (train)	*tee-eh loo*	tiě lù 铁 路
trade fair	*shahng peen - jee-aow ee hway*	shāng pǐn 商 品 jiāo yì huì 交 易 会
trade, commerce	*maow ee*	mào yì 贸 易
trademark	*shahng bee-aow*	shāng biāo 商 标
traffic light	*hohng liew dung*	hóng lù dēng 红 绿 灯
traffic	*jee-aow tohng*	jiāo tōng 交 通
train station	*hwuh chuh jahn*	huǒ chē zhàn 火 车 站
train	*hwuh chuh*	huǒ chē 火 车
transaction	*jee-aow ee*	jiāo yì 交 易
transfer (bank)	*jwahn jahng*	zhuǎn zhǎng 转 账

transfer money	*hway kwahn*	huì kuǎn 汇 款
translate	*fahn ee*	fān yì 翻 译
translator	*fahn ee*	fān yì 翻 译
transportation	*ywun shoo*	yùn shū 运 输
trash bin	*lah jee - shee-ahng*	lā jī xiāng 垃 圾 箱
travel agency	*liew shing shuh*	lǚ xíng shè 旅 行 社
travel, trip	*liew shing*	lǚ xíng 旅 行
traveler's check	*liew shing - jir pee-aow*	lǚ xíng zhī piào 旅 行 支 票
treatment (medical)	*jir lee-aow*	zhì liáo 治 疗
tree	*shoo*	shù 树
trousers	*koo zih*	kù zǐ 裤 子
truck	*kah chuh*	kǎ chē 卡 车
T-shirt	*tee shiew shahn*	xù shān T 恤 衫
Tsingtao beer	*Ching daow - pee jeo*	Qīng dǎo pí jiǔ 青 岛 啤 酒
Tuesday	*Shing chee ar*	xīng qī èr 星 期 二
tuition	*shweh fay*	xué fèi 学 费

tunnel	*sway daow*	suì dào 隧道
turkey (bird)	*hwuh jee*	huǒ jī 火鸡
Turkey (country)	*Too ar chee*	Tǔ ěr qí 土耳其
turn off (switch)	*gwahn*	guān 关
turn on (switch)	*dah kye*	dǎ kāi 打开
turn (change direction)	*jwahn wahn*	zhuǎn wān 转弯
turtle	*woo gway*	wū guī 乌龟
tutor	*jee-ah jee-aow*	jiā jiào 家教
TV	*dee-en shir*	diàn shì 电视
tweezers	*nee-eh zih*	niè zi 镊子
twelve	*shir ar*	shí èr 十二
twenty	*ar shir*	èr shí 二十
two	*ar* or *lee-ahng*	èr liǎng 二；两
type (write)	*dah zih*	dǎ zì 打字
type, kind	*johng lay*	zhǒng lèi 种类
typewriter	*dah zih jee*	dǎ zì jī 打字机

typhoon	*tye fung*	tái fēng 台 风
typhus	*shahng hahn*	shāng hán 伤 寒
typist	*dah zih ywahn*	dǎ zì yuán 打 字 员
ugly	*nahn kahn duh*	nán kàn de 难 看 的
ulcer	*kway yahng*	kuì yáng 溃 疡
umbrella	*yiew sahn*	yǔ sǎn 雨 伞
unacceptable	*boo nung -* *jee-eh shoh duh*	bù néng 不 能 jiē shòu de 接 受 的
uncle	*shoo shoo*	shū shu 叔 叔
uncomfortable	*boo shoo foo - duh*	bù shū fu de 不 舒 服 的
uncooked	*shung duh*	shēng de 生 的
understand	*ming bye* or *lee jee-eh*	míng bai 明 白 ; lǐ jiě 理 解
underwear	*nay ee*	nèi yī 内 衣
unemployed	*shir yee-eh duh*	shī yè de 失 业 的
unhappy	*boo gaow shing- duh*	bù gāo xìng de 不 高 兴 的

uniform	*jir foo*	zhì fú 制 服
unique	*doo tuh duh*	dú tè de 独 特 的
unit, team	*dahn way*	dān wèi 单 位
United Nations	*Lee-en huh - gwuh*	Lián hé guó 联 合 国
United States	*May gwuh*	Měi guó 美 国
university	*dah shweh*	dà xué 大 学
upper	*shahng mee-en - duh*	shàng mian de 上 面 的
upstairs	*loh shahng*	lóu shàng 楼 上
urgent matter	*jee shir*	jí shì 急 事
urinate	*shee-aow bee-en*	xiǎo biàn 小 便
urine	*nee-aow*	niào 尿
us	*wuh men*	wǒ men 我 们
use	*yohng*	yòng 用
vacation	*jee-ah chee*	jià qī 假 期
vaccination certificate	*fahng ee jung*	fáng yì zhèng 防 疫 证

vagina	*yeen daow*	yīn dào 阴道
valley	*shahn goo*	shān gǔ 山 谷
valuable	*yoh jee-ah - jir duh*	yǒu jià zhí de 有 价 值 的
value	*jee-ah jir*	jià zhí 价 值
Vancouver	*Wen guh hwah*	Wēn gē huá 温 哥 华
vegetable	*shoo tsye*	shū cài 蔬 菜
vegetarian	*soo shir juh*	sù shí zhě 素 食 者
vehicle	*chuh lee-ahng*	chē liàng 车 辆
venereal disease	*shing bing*	xìng bìng 性 病
very	*hen* or	hěn 很 ;
	fay chahng	fēi cháng 非 常
vest	*bay sheen*	bèi xīn 背 心
video camera	*shuh ying jee*	shè yǐng jī 摄 影 机
Vietnam	*Yweh nahn*	Yuè nán 越 南
view (verb)	*kahn*	kàn 看
view, scenery	*jing suh*	jǐng sè 景 色

village	*tswun jwahng*	cūn zhuāng 村 庄
vinegar	*tsoo*	cù 醋
visa	*chee-en jung*	qiān zhèng 签 证
visa extension	*yahn chahng -* *chee-en jung*	yán cháng 延 长 qiān zhèng 签 证
visit (a person)	*bye fahng*	bài fǎng 拜 访
visit (a place)	*tsahn gwahn*	cān guān 参 观
visitor, guest	*lye fahng juh*	lái fǎng zhě 来 访 者
visitor, tourist	*yoh kuh*	yóu kè 游 客
vocabulary	*tsih hway*	cí huì 词 汇
vodka	*foo tuh jee-ah*	fú tè jiā 伏 特 加
voice	*shung yeen*	shēng yīn 声 音
volleyball	*pye cheo*	pái qiú 排 球
voltage	*wah*	wǎ 瓦
vomit	*oh too*	ǒu tù 呕 吐
vote	*toh pee-aow*	tóu piào 投 票

wage, salary	*sheen shway*	xīn shuǐ 薪 水
waist	*yaow*	yāo 腰
wait	*dung*	děng 等
waiter, waitress	*foo woo ywahn*	fú wù yuán 服 务 员
wake up	*shing lye*	xǐng lái 醒 来
walk	*zoh*	zǒu 走
wall	*chee-ahng*	qiáng 墙
wallet	*chee-en baow*	qián bāo 钱 包
want	*shee-ahng*	xiǎng 想
war	*jahn jung*	zhàn zhēng 战 争
warm	*nwahn hwuh*	nuǎn huo 暖 和
wash, clean	*shee*	xǐ 洗
washbasin	*lee-en pen*	liǎn pén 脸 盆
washing machine	*shee ee jee*	xǐ yī jī 洗 衣 机
Washington	*Hwah shung - dwun*	Huá shèng dùn 华 盛 顿
wastebasket	*fay jir loh*	fèi zhǐ lǒu 废 纸 篓

wastepaper	*fay jir*	fèi zhǐ 废 纸
watch (rerb)	*kahn*	kàn 看
water (noun)	*shway*	shuǐ 水
waterfall	*poo boo*	pù bù 瀑 布
watermelon	*shee gwah*	xī guā 西 瓜
waterproof	*fahng shway*	fáng shuǐ 防 水
water-ski	*hwah shway*	huá shuǐ 滑 水
wave (sea)	*hye lahng*	hǎi làng 海 浪
way (method)	*fahng fah*	fāng fǎ 方 法
way out (exit)	*choo koh*	chū kǒu 出 口
we	*wuh men*	wǒ men 我 们
weak (not strong)	*rwuh*	ruò 弱
wealthy	*foo yoh duh*	fù yǒu de 富 有 的
weather forecast	*tee-en chee - yiew baow*	tiān qì yù bào 天 气 预 报
weather	*tee-en chee*	tiān qì 天 气
wedding	*hwun lee*	hūn lǐ 婚 礼

Wednesday	*Shing chee sahn*	xīng qī sān 星 期 三
week	*shing chee*	xīng qī 星 期
weekend	*joh mwuh*	zhōu mò 周 末
weigh	*chung ___*	chēng 称 ___
weight	*johng lee-ahng*	zhòng liàng 重 量
weird	*gwye ee duh*	guài yì de 怪 异 的
welcome	*hwahn ying*	huān yíng 欢 迎
well (good)	*haow*	hǎo 好
west	*shee bee-en*	xī biān 西 边
western country	*shee fahng - gwuh jee-ah*	xī fāng guó jiā 西 方 国 家
western food	*shee tsahn*	xī cān 西 餐
western medicine	*shee yaow*	xī yào 西 药
western toilet	*zwuh bee-en - chee*	zuò biàn qì 坐 便 器
western	*shee fahng duh*	xī fāng de 西 方 的
westerner	*shee fahng ren*	xī fāng rén 西 方 人
westernized	*shee fahng - hwah duh*	xī fāng huà de 西 方 化 的

wet	*shir*	shī 湿
what	*shen muh*	shén me 什 么
wheat flour	*mee-en fen*	miàn fěn 面 粉
when	*shen muh - shir hoh*	shén me shí hòu 什 么 时 候
where	*nah lee*	nǎ li 哪 里
which	*nah ee guh*	nǎ yí gè 哪 一 个
while	*dahng ___ - shir hoh*	dāng shí hòu 当 ___时 候
whisky	*way shir jee*	wēi shì jì 威 士 忌
who	*shway*	shuí 谁
wholesale	*pee fah*	pī fā 批 发
why	*way shen muh*	wèi shén me 为 什 么
wide, broad	*kwahn*	kuān 宽
wife	*chee zih, laow pwuh* or *tye tye*	qī zǐ lǎo pó 妻 子； 老 婆； tài tai 太 太
wild animal	*yee-eh shung - dohng woo*	yě shēng dòng wù 野 生 动 物
will (verb)	*jee-ahng yaow*	jiāng yào 将 要

wind	*fung*	fēng 风
windmill	*fung chuh*	fēng chē 风 车
window	*chwahng hoo*	chuāng hù 窗 户
windy	*fung hen - dah duh*	fēng hěn dà de 风 很 大 的
wine	*poo taow jeo*	pú tao jiǔ 葡 萄 酒
winter	*dohng tee-en*	dōng tiān 冬 天
wish	*shee wahng*	xī wàng 希 望
with	*gen___*	gēn 跟 ___
withdraw	*chiew chee-en*	qǔ qián 取 钱
without	*may yoh*	méi yǒu 没 有
wok	*gwuh*	guō 锅
wolf	*lahng*	láng 狼
woman	*niew ren*	nǚ rén 女 人
wood	*moo toh*	mù tou 木 头
woods	*shoo leen*	shù lín 树 林
wool	*yahng maow*	yáng máo 羊 毛

word	*tsih*	cí 词
work (noun & verb)	*gohng zwuh*	gōng zuò 工作
worker	*gohng ren*	gōng rén 工人
workshop	*yahn taow kuh*	yán tǎo kè 研讨课
world	*shir jee-eh*	shì jiè 世界
worm	*chohng zih*	chóng zi 虫子
worrisome	*ling ren -* *dahn sheen duh*	lìng rén 令人 dān xīn de 担心的
worship	*chohng bye*	chóng bài 崇拜
wound	*shahng koh*	shāng kǒu 伤口
wrap	*baow*	bāo 包
wrist	*shoh wahn*	shǒu wàn 手腕
wristwatch	*shoh bee-aow*	shǒu biǎo 手表
write	*shee-eh*	xiě 写
writer	*zwuh juh*	zuò zhě 作者
writing paper	*sheen jir*	xìn zhǐ 信纸

written language	*shoo mee-en - yiew*	shū miàn yǔ 书 面 语
wrong	*tswuh duh*	cuò de 错 的
Xi'an	*Shee ahn*	Xī ān 西 安
Xinjiang	*Sheen jee-ahng*	Xīn jiāng 新 疆
X-ray	*X gwahng*	guāng X 光
Yangtse River	*Chahng - jee-ahng*	Cháng jiāng 长 江
yard (measurement)	*mah*	mǎ 码
yard, courtyard	*ywahn zih*	yuàn zi 院 子
year	*nee-en*	nián 年
yearly	*may nee-en*	měi nián 每 年
Yellow River	*Hwahng huh*	Huáng hé 黄 河
yellow	*hwahng suh*	huáng sè 黄 色
yes	*shir*	shì 是
yesterday	*zwuh tee-en*	zuó tiān 昨 天
yogurt	*swahn nye*	suān nǎi 酸 奶
you (plural)	*nee men*	nǐ men 你 们

you	*nee*	nǐ 你
young	*nee-en ching*	nián qīng 年 轻
your	*nee duh*	nǐ de 你 的
your (plural)	*nee men duh*	nǐ men de 你 们 的
yours	*nee duh* or *nee men duh*	nǐ de 你 的 ; nǐ men de 你 们 的
yourself	*nee zih jee*	nǐ zì jǐ 你 自 己
youth	*nee-en ching- ren*	nián qīng rén 年 轻 人
zero	*ling*	líng 零
zipper	*lah lee-en*	lā liàn 拉 链
zoo	*dohng woo- ywahn*	dòng wù yuán 动 物 园

沧海一粟

A drop in the ocean.
Tsahng hye ee soo.

鲁迅先生说过："无情未必真豪杰，怜子如何不丈夫?"

　　这句话，令我感同身受．关爱那些您也许永远不认识或不会见面的孩子们，这一点意义非同寻常．这就是我与"联合国儿童基金会"合作的意义所在．您也可以同样提供您的帮助．购买"联合国儿童基金会"的贺卡．把它寄给您的亲朋好友－会有更多的中国儿童得到帮助。

　　请今年邮寄"联合国儿童基金会"的贺卡．将您的爱心传递给更多的人。

　　让我们共同帮助建设一个适合儿童生长的世界。

成龙
联合国儿童基金会亲善大使

The Chinese writer Lu Xun wrote that heartlessness is no prerequisite for heroism and that loving children is no barrier to becoming a real man.

Take it from me, caring for Chinese children you'll never get to know or even meet can be as good as caring gets. That's why I'm working with UNICEF and that's why you can help, too.
Every UNICEF card you buy and send means more children can be helped by UNICEF's projects right here in China.

Please send UNICEF cards this year and send a message of kindness to those you most care about.

Let's work with UNICEF to help build a World Fit For Children.

Jackie Chan
UNICEF Goodwill Ambassador

欢迎垂询，请致电：010-65323131 转 2207
For more information,please call:010-65323131 ext 2207

Printed in the United States
97505LV00004B/1-45/A